Homework Heroes

Drew and Cynthia Johnson

with Introduction by

Priscilla L. Vail, M. A. T.

KAPLAN BOOKS

New York   London   Toronto   Sydney   Singapore

Kaplan Publishing
Published by Simon & Schuster, Inc.
1230 Avenue of the Americas
New York, NY 10020

For bulk sales to schools, colleges, and universities, please contact: Order Department, Simon & Schuster, Inc., 100 Front Street, Riverside, NJ 08075. Phone: (800) 223-2336. Fax: (800) 943-9831.

For information regarding special discounts for other bulk purchases, please contact Simon & Schuster Special Sales at 1-800-456-6798 or business@simonandschuster.com

Editor: Beth Grupper
Cover Design: Cheung Tai
Interior Design: Richard Oriolo
Interior Layout and Production: Anaxos, Inc.

Manufactured in the United States of America

January 2002
10 9 8 7 6 5 4 3 2 1

Library of Congress Cataloging-in-Publication Data

ISBN: 0-7432-2257-1

Table of Contents

Chapter 3: A Review of Basic K-2 English Concepts

Chapter 4: A Review of Basic K-2 Science and

  Social Studies Concepts

Homework Heroes:
Grades K-2

 HOMEWORK IS A FACT OF life for most children, but parents are often confused about their role in this daily drama and concerned about meshing homework with the general dynamics of personal and family life. While homework sometimes causes frustration and arguments for you and your child, it can also be a vehicle for cooperation, a source of pride and accomplishment, and an opportunity for fun and creativity.

Fantasy? No.

From my own experiences as a full-time teacher for over a quarter of a century, a parent of four children, a grandmother of six, a student of learning, a curriculum planner, and a designer and leader of teacher and parenting workshops across this country and abroad, I have some:

complexities to explore and strategies to share

cautions to mention and techniques to offer

issues to highlight and research to quarry

questions to raise and purposes to reinforce

By exploring these combinations you and your child can enhance the positive aspects of this daily reality. You can be Homework Heroes to one another. The second section of this book offers additional nuts and bolts to set you on your way.

If you have read some of my books or articles, or have heard me speak, some of what follows here may sound familiar. Good, that means we are already friends. For new acquaintances, my message is both realistic and optimistic:

Your child can succeed.

You can survive.

There is life after homework.

Consolidation and Confidence

The goal of homework in kindergarten through second grade is to help students *consolidate* what they have learned in school, and gain *confidence* in themselves as independent learners. These are twin foundations for later learning, and now is the time to help them grow sturdy.

Students at this age usually think homework is cool, a badge of maturity and honor. In fact, children this age often invent their own if the teacher doesn't assign any!

Ideally, official assignments are simple, fun, and designed with success in mind. After all, if homework is to be an introduction to independence, reliability, and responsibility, adults should help children feel that this yoke is easy and light, so they will wear it willingly in the future.

Here's a truth: children this age move from *learning to love* to *loving to learn*. Young children grow through establishing bonds with others. First they love a person, then they broaden that love to include what that person offers or teaches. Affectionate, empathetic teachers magnetize young learners. Children in kindergarten through second grade often, literally, fall in love with their teachers, and then they reach out for the information and knowledge that a teacher offers. In older children, the subject matter is the draw, but at this age it is the person. Your child already loves you. If you, in addition to being center stage in your child's life, approach learning with joy and curiosity, you will soon find your child embracing learning in the same way.

Here are twenty questions to address in thinking about homework. This structure can provide a banister to support and guide us as we walk our way up through this important, sometimes conflict-ridden topic.

1. What is the homework policy at your child's school?

2. What is each teacher's homework policy?

3. What is your homework policy as a parent?

4. Who has ownership of homework?

5. How does homework solidify or undermine eight homework relationships?

6. Time: Does your child use it well?

7. Space: Where is homework to be done?

8. Do you have a Time and Space Homework Pact?

9. How long should homework take?

10. What about boredom and drudgery?

11. Does your child have the prerequisite reading skills to manage assigned homework?

12. Do your child's developmental and language levels match the assigned tasks?

13. Do your child's handwriting skills match the assigned tasks?

14. Do your child's study skills and learning styles match the assigned tasks?

15. What if your child has dyslexia or a learning disability?

16. Are your child's emotional habits and considerations taken into account?

17. Does your child's memory capacity match the expectations of the homework?

18. Does the homework attach new concepts to ones that are already familiar?

19. Does your child's homework promote privacy, participation, and enjoying your kid?

20. Do you watch the "Plimsoll Line"? (No it's not a new television show. Puzzled? Read on.)

Let's look at these twenty questions, one by one, and explore their implications for children from kindergarten through second grade.

1. What is the homework policy at your child's school?

If homework is going to demand the amount of time schools expect and require, the school philosophy should be clear and articulated. Is homework for

reinforcement of concepts?

extension of concepts?

preparation for concepts?

development of independent learning?

enjoyment and expansion of creativity?

drill and practice, including test preparation?

time filling?

You have every right to ask for, encourage, or even demand a statement from the school on its homework philosophy. If such a statement is not in place, or in writing, it is reasonable to ask the administration when they would be able to have one ready: next week, next month, three months? What would they like you and other parents to do in the meantime? Parents (and students) deserve this information.

Since many schools have not articulated a homework policy, it may take a little time and "cajoling," but never underestimate the power a coordinated group wields. Be polite but firm, remembering that schools, like most institutions, move at a glacial pace.

2. What is each teacher's homework policy?

Are each teacher's ideas consistent with what the school has stated, and among each other? Do all first grade teachers give the same amount of homework or is one a task master, one a softie, and still another governed by whim and mood?

Young children remain in self-contained classrooms for most of their school time; therefore, they usually have one head teacher who makes the decisions. In later grades, they will have many teachers, but for now one is the norm. Usually the homeroom teacher will outline the homework policy on back-to-school night or in a newsletter sent home early in the year. Otherwise, most teachers will be glad to answer individual parent questions on the topic.

A teacher who has not thought through this issue needs to do so.

A tactful query from a parent may do the trick. If not, a little help from the administration is in order, but always try talking to the teacher first.

3. What is your homework policy as a parent?

How should assignments fit with the life of the home? After all, it is called *homework;* home priorities should figure in!

At this level, you can dignify your child's homework obligations while keeping them in proportion. Remember that the goals of homework in the earliest grades are consolidation and confidence; try to keep enjoyment, a sense of accomplishment, and pride alive. For example, one family kept an index card with the words "All Done!" on the refrigerator door. Each child had a personal magnet. When the homework was done, the child could put his dog or lighthouse or superhero magnet on the card. Public triumph!

Put your family's habits and priorities into words, and talk about how they fit together with homework. "In this family, we all eat dinner together. Homework must be done before we eat." The important thing is to put it into words so everyone understands.

The same is true of bedtime. Spell out the combination of homework and downtime. "In our family, each child has a separate bedtime. But all children in this family must have their homework finished fifteen minutes before tooth brushing time."

This, of course, requires that you have decided on family patterns and put them into words. If you were accustomed to spur-of-the-moment living before you had children, you may not have taken this step. But you need to do it now. School age children need structure, and no, it won't inhibit their creativity.

4. Who has ownership of homework?

Let there be no fuzziness here: your child owns, and is responsible for, the assignments; your child is the one to do the work. Thus, your child will own the triumphs. Anything else is theft.

Does this mean no help? Of course not. While it is not up to you to finish a science project or complete an arithmetic sheet, you should help by providing the time and space in which to work on assignments, offering encouragement, listening to spelling words, admiring a product, praising diligence, helping to sound out an unfamiliar word, or running through flash cards for arithmetic. Yes, you should be interested and supportive, but the ownership of the homework belongs to the child.

5. How does homework solidify or undermine eight homework relationships?

parent/child	child/parent
parent/teacher	child/teacher
parent/family	child/family
parent/self	child/self

Understanding how these relationships interconnect, and being sure all are in good repair, separately and jointly, is fundamental to effective vigilance, your privilege as a parent.

In the **parent/child** homework relationship, your opportunities are seven: dignify the child's labors, guarantee a suitable setting for the work, let the child do the work, admire the effort and the product, provide a homework checklist, help the child establish productive work habits, and, above all, model the behaviors you expect from your kid.

In the **child/parent** homework relationship, you want your child to establish feelings of responsibility, diligence without dependency, and pride in accomplishment. This means that you will sometimes need to step out of the way even if you know that you could paste the picture onto the page more evenly. This takes self-control. Restraint can be as hard to cultivate as patience, but your child will reap rewards of autonomy.

In the **parent/teacher** homework relationship, you should be friendly and supportive, yet honest when there is a problem. If an assignment is stressful for your child, or takes too long, state it in a "we" message. "We had trouble last night getting the work done in twenty minutes. How can you help us?" This is less apt to provoke a defensive reaction than, "Your assignment was too long."

When talking over homework issues with a teacher, start by making yourself an ally, not an adversary. Mention something positive about the class: "Susie so enjoyed hearing you read *The Deadly Dragon*, and told us all about the picture storyboard the class created." Then you can move to the problem, being descriptive instead of critical, and ask for a team approach in solving it. Remember, teachers have feelings, too.

An inside tip for parents: *never* pounce on a teacher in the hall or at the door of the classroom as the day is starting. The teacher's proper focus is on the group: orchestrating the day, drawing the group into the lesson, generating excitement, soothing feelings, and infusing courage. Diverting the teacher's concentration away at such a time is like delivering a telephone message to a golfer on his backswing. Instead, send a note saying what you want to talk about, how much time you need, and suggest a date and time, or ask the teacher to set an alternative.

In the **child/teacher** homework relationship, the child needs to be totally honest with the teacher: "I loved that project" or "My hand gets too tired to write that much" or "I don't like to read." You may need to help your child put the problem into words and provide an opportunity to practice how to say those words to the teacher. When your child is honest, the teacher can do what teachers go into teaching to do: help.

In the **parent/family** homework relationship, you need to help each child coordinate individual homework demands with the competing needs of siblings, spouse, the dog, or a grandparent. (Being a grandparent myself allows me to use that sequence.)

You need to be calm and fair in distributing your time, attention, and moral support where they are needed, while remembering that, since you are human, there is a limit. Often simply saying, "There's only one of me. I'll do my best, but I also need to make the salad and call the dentist," may be enough. Sometimes you may have to spell out what resources you can give to which person or project. You should not feel guilty that you can't be everywhere for everyone. You should not feel like road kill.

In the **child/family** homework relationship, insofar as possible, each child should do assignments, with their attendant demands for help, quiet, and so forth, when others in the family are similarly engaged. Thus, each child in a family should have an ample supply of quiet, enjoyable projects to do solo while others are still working.

In the **parent/self** relationship, you should get a life! I mean this in the nicest way. Be gentle with yourself. Remember the comment above about road kill. Yoga, music, athletics, computers, and opportunities for adult companionship are nourishing to the spirit, and, by the way, good for physical health. Such activities provide refreshing breaks which replenish your energies, not to mention your sense of humor. Do not let your life be devoured by your child's homework. Well-intentioned parents who fall into this trap often build dependence, instead of autonomy, in their children.

In the **child/self** relationship, your child should learn to behave responsibly, feel proud, be honest about what is hard and what is easy, and enjoy successes—homework included. This means you have to spend some private, reflective time with your child (each child) at the end of the day. Be sure to slot this in to the family schedule. Don't skip it! Self monitoring is a vital life-long skill. Your child needs to start developing it now.

6. Time: Does your child use it well?

Human beings use time for planning, charting, and monitoring their work and their play. Planning requires a sense of past, present, and future. Kids need to understand these concepts in order to succeed in school and on assignments.

First, be sure your child can tell time, using an analog watch and clock as well as digital timepieces. Why? A digital timepiece shows only the present moment, giving no indication of what came before or what is around the corner. It is important to consolidate this now, teaching this skill if necessary. A solid concept of time, including a sense of the passing of time (technically called *elapsing time*) has a benevolent effect on your child's academic future.

You, yourself, should try to speak in concise time language: "It's 5:15 now. You need to start your homework in fifteen minutes," or "We have ten minutes until supper. Do you want to throw the ball around?"

You can also help your child by using precise names for times of the day, days of the week, months of the year, holidays, and seasons, avoiding the imprecise "later on," "a while ago," "someday soon," or the urgent and non-specific, "Hurry up. We're late!"

Internalizing such concepts as "first," "next," and "finally" helps your child construct sequences. These may pinch the pernicious habit of procrastination in the bud.

Having the precise language of time and sequence allows your child to file and sort experiences, develop a personal timeline, and thus become, in effect, the curator of his own life.

The Time and Space Homework Pact described under question 8 lays out a specific way for you and your child to plan homework.

7. Space: Where is the homework to be done?

It is important for you and your child to identify, guarantee, and equip a place for your child to work, even giving it a name: Homework Heaven, the Studying Spot, or the Serious Desk. Your child should establish the habit of going there to do homework, leaving when the job is done. It should *not* be in front of the television! It is important for you and your child to acknowledge that surroundings influence concentration and focus . . . as well as their opposites. Some places are designed for fun and relaxation. Even children this young can learn to choose their settings according to their purposes. The following section offers some suggestions for choosing a homework location.

8. Do you have a Time and Space Homework Pact?

Time and space are the foundations of what I call Sheridan's Tyranny, a tongue-in-cheek name for wisdom from the late Harriet Sheridan, Dean at Carleton College, and then at Brown University. She said that the distinguishing feature between students who succeed in college and those who fall by the wayside is the ability to organize themselves in time and space. This skill, she pointed out, is vital in college, necessary in high school, supportive in middle school, helpful in elementary school, and comforting in kindergarten.

If it's that beneficial at that many levels, she emphasized, it's only common sense to start developing it as early as possible, and keep it going all the way through.

These comments led to what I call the Time and Space Homework Pact.

Even at this young age, it is important for you and your child to settle on a family policy of *when* and *where* homework is to be done. Older children need to make a formal pact with their parents, but, at this level, simply talking specifically about times and places for homework, making verbal agreements—and sticking to them—is sufficient.

Factor in your child's preferences and the family realities.

First, let's discuss the time component of the pact. Your child may want to sit right down after school and polish off the homework. Or your child may need to have something to eat, play with the guinea pig, skip rope, or log on to the computer for a while before revisiting academics. If your child has an after-school activity on Tuesdays and Thursdays, he may need to have supper first on those evenings and then tackle homework. Your child's individual needs and preferences count and must be part of the pact, or it will feel more repressive than supportive.

Now let's think about the space component of the pact. Your child may like to do homework in the bedroom. But, if your child is like many others, the bedroom has connotations of drifting and dreaming. That atmosphere may override the purposefulness studying requires. If so, your child may study better in the living room, the den, or at the kitchen table. No single answer is right for all children. Consider both your home environment and your child's preferences.

When all the issues have been fleshed out, you and your child need to agree on the terms of the pact. Everyone should understand that the agreement will stand for six weeks. After that, all issues can be renegotiated. During those six weeks, however, there will be no further discussion of the whens and wheres. This fair and comprehensive approach eliminates nightly bargaining, which is a great relief to all concerned.

If you want a written pact for children this age, a sample follows:

Homework time starts at 5:00, and will continue uninterrupted until complete. There will be time for a snack before starting, and time to play when it is finished. Homework will be done at the dining room table, which will be free of clutter.

This pact will remain in effect until _____(date).
Signed: _____
(your child)

_____
(you)
Date:_____

Post the pact on the refrigerator, the family bulletin board, or some other serious, public place.

Needless to say, it is only fair to expect parents to model the behaviors they expect from their children. If you have promised that a clear work surface in the kitchen will be ready when your child comes home from school, you can't say, "Oh, I forgot. Let's do the homework later . . . in the car."

Caution: some parents have adopted what I call "Ragamuffin Chic," an attitude that grunge is cute, lateness is evidence of innocence, and dirty fingernails indicate freedom from repression. If you as a parent feel this way yourself, and encourage your child in such attitudes, you undermine your own goals of having successful, happy children who can cooperate, laugh, and get the job done at an appropriate level. At the risk of sounding Victorian, you can learn to be organized and prompt just as well as children can, and you must do so if you want the best for them.

9. How long should homework take?

Many thoughtful schools have adopted the rule of thumb that there should be ten minutes per night per grade level: ten minutes for first-graders, twenty for second-graders.

Kindergarteners should have one small project if anything. For example, an appropriate assignment for a kindergartener might be: "Practice writing your name the way you have been taught in school. Please bring in five signatures," or "Bring in a picture of something that starts with the sound /s/."

Even if your child's school has adopted a rule of thumb, you (and they) need to remember that children this age work at very different paces, so a rule of thumb should be a guideline, not an ironclad policy.

If the assignments are too hard, or take too long, you, or you and your child together, should talk with the teacher, being open and honest as suggested in the discussion of question 5.

You, as the parent, should monitor the amount of time spent on homework, set limits, and protect your child.

10. What about boredom and drudgery?

Boredom: is it phony or real? Sometimes, to save face, children say, "I'm bored," or "This is boring," when they really mean, "I'm scared I can't do this," or "This is too hard."

In my first year of teaching, I had a red-headed first-grade girl who would flip through her reader, shouting out "I'm finished. This book is a bore!" For a little while, I was fooled, and spent hours trying to find materials that matched her arcane interests. She would tell me she only wanted to read about "insects of ancient Egypt" and I would scurry off to the library. Finally, I recognized the camouflage and followed the advice of an experienced teacher who said, "Sit down with her and say, 'We're going to figure out these words together. Now.'"

In cases of simulated boredom, the trick is to get right at the problem, break down the task, and help with whatever components are getting in the way. The longer the masquerade continues, the harder it is to get the real, necessary job done.

Real boredom is a problem when teachers assign numerous worksheets of tasks the child has already mastered. In such cases, you might say to the teacher, "Sam is very good at addition, but gets bogged down if he has to do fifty problems a night. Would it be possible for him to do every other problem, or half the problems and use the extra time for a project? Perhaps he could use more time on other areas in which he needs help?"

Drudgery is a necessary part of some kinds of learning: you can't learn a new language without memorizing new vocabulary. If your child is slogging through a repetitive task, see whether it is preliminary to higher-level knowledge or whether it is just a dismal time-filler. One is a necessary evil, the other is an evil unnecessary.

You and your child can figure this out together, or ask the teacher tactfully.

11. Does your child have the prerequisite reading skills to manage assigned homework?

In order to understand whether your child has the prerequisite reading skills for the homework, you need to see how reading prowess unfolds.

Reading levels progress this way:

Emergent reading: understanding what reading is, recognizing a few words

Early reading: being able to sound out words or string words together in short sentences

Con'-tent reading: getting information and plot from reading

Con-tent' reading: relaxed, accurate intake; fluency; use of punctuation for phrasing

Nimble reading: moving easily among factual, survey, and aesthetic reading

Students in kindergarten through second grade usually master emergent and early reading. Some first graders and many second graders are also con'-tent readers.

For obvious reasons, assignments, whether they are in language arts, social studies, or math, must match the child's reading level.

To get going, your child needs to have such prerequisite skills as:

the ability to recognize some words by sight

the ability to decode words (sound them out)

the ability to encode words (spell them)

the ability to transcode words (converting individual words and sentences into meaning)

Here are some things to notice as you monitor your child's reading skills.

Perhaps, even as a preschooler, your child could read labels on food packages. If so, your child was recognizing words by their shape and size, perhaps even color. This is reading by sight. Many early readers are sight readers.

This is an exciting ability, but your child still needs to learn to sound out words by knowing what sounds the letters make, or to use the technical term, *decoding*. As a parent, you can assess your child's knowledge of phonics by making up short nonsense words for her to read. If letter/sound knowledge is skimpy or non-existent, get help.

Children reinforce decoding skills, as well as learn to spell, by running the process in reverse. The technical term for this is *encoding*. Decoding and encoding, along with handwriting, are best taught together in what is called *multisensory* instruction, sometimes called the Orton/Gillingham method. As a parent, you can play with this idea by giving your child a word and seeing whether she can tell you the beginning sound, the last sound, or the sound in the middle. By late kindergarten, most children can do this. Can your child count the number of sounds in the word *c-a-t*? Most first graders can. Can your child count and say the sounds in the word *f-l-a-g* or *l-a-s-t*? Most second graders can. Can your child attach letters to the sounds and put them in order to make *c-a-t, f-l-a-g,* or *l-a-s-t*?

Here's a caution for you as a parent: some schools do not believe in teaching "sounding out." If your child hasn't been taught these techniques, and can't perform these tasks, you may want to procure some outside help. Without getting into the quicksand of reading instruction controversy, it is fair to say that the research indicates the importance of knowing how to do the above.

As children decode and encode, we also need to be sure they can transcode, or attach meaning to the squiggles on the page and the individual words coming out of their mouths. Transcoding is the connective tissue of reading and writing.

If your child can read a sentence, a page, a small book, or a fat one, does she know what was happening to the characters on the page? Can she describe the mean man, the wicked troll, or can she tell why the little boy climbed a string to a cloud to escape from danger? These aren't extraneous questions. Sometimes children can lift words off the page and spout them quickly, but have no idea what stories or ideas they convey.

As a parent, you can bolster transcoding in a lighthearted way. For example, while driving in the car or riding on the bus, see how many synonyms you and your child can brainstorm for *moving* (*running, jumping, skipping,* etc.), or *making sounds* (*yelling, clattering, whining,* etc.). You can also take turns with one of you saying a word and the other making up a story based on that word, such as *dragon, cave,* or *tightly-covered box.*

12. Do your child's developmental and language levels match the assigned tasks?

You can't make the grass grow by pulling it. In fact, you risk yanking it out. The same idea applies to children's developmental levels, not simply in early childhood but all the way to adulthood. Actually, common knowledge now tells us that adults have their developmental progressions, too.

For the child to be successful, academic tasks and developmental levels must match. Children tell us a great deal about their developmental level by their humor and their literary appetites. For example, most kindergarteners relish stories of people or animals who can't resist misbehaving. Guess why? They're looking in the mirror. Curious George is a kindergartener's relief act. He makes them feel superior, since they would never do *that*!

First-graders gravitate to stories in which the small overcomes the large. Guess why? Such stories are gateways to hope. When the youngest sister snags the prince and the kingdom, when the third son rides the stallion to the top of the glass hill to collect the golden apples from the lap of the princess, and earns all the subsequent rewards, the little first-grader feels stirrings of optimism. First-graders also gobble up stories dealing with what's fair and unfair. Guess why? When you're small, without even a full mouthful of teeth, the world doesn't always take you seriously.

Second-graders like silliness and solemnity. They roar over Amelia Bedelia, a favorite children's book character who, when asked to dust the furniture, shakes dust on the chairs and tables. They also like to amass such serious items as compound words and the technical names of dinosaurs. Guess why? They catch on to verbal jokes, and they are ready to start cataloging.

Knowledge of developmental levels allows parents and teachers to coordinate reading and assignments with the child's natural interest level. Bingo! But what if the homework doesn't jibe?

For example, second-graders (and younger children) aren't ready to write research papers, they are ready to write stories. If a teacher assigns your second grader a paper on an explorer, ask the teacher whether you and your child can read the basic information together. Then ask your child to tell you about the explorer as if it were a story. Ask your child to make some illustrations and together make some captions.

How can you tell when your child is developmentally overwhelmed? Children who freeze at an assignment may prefer paralysis to failure. Children who say, "This is boring," as we saw above, may be in over their heads.

Children who hand in a "factory outlet" level response to an assignment may be saying, "I'm not ready for these subtleties or nuances."

Bright children who appear thick-headed may be those who Anthony Bashir, a Boston-based linguist and educator, was talking about when he explained that "When we give children work to do which is developmentally beyond them, they punish us by showing us how dumb they are."

If your child is assigned developmentally inappropriate homework, talk to the teacher and see whether you can adjust the expectations as shown in the explorer example above. The trick is to leave the concepts intact but scale back the expectations, break the information down into small and manageable bits, and shorten the required output.

Remember, children develop at different paces, particularly during their first years in school. Your child may enjoy Amelia Bedelia earlier or later than indicated above. Your kindergartener

Sometimes there are external indicators of internal developmental levels. For example, in many cases (though not all), children catch on to reading at about the same time they lose their baby teeth. When the new choppers begin to descend, it is as though moving from dental babyhood to maturity coordinates with moving from literary immaturity to literary competence. This isn't always true, but I've seen it happen enough that it's worth including here. This does not mean that if your child is struggling with reading you can say, "Oh, we'll just wait for those teeth." Struggling readers need help as soon as possible, but the nature of the help must be on par with the child.

may want to put Curious George on the bottom shelf, or your second-grader may want to take him to bed. Listen to what your own child tells you.

Although developmental levels and language levels intertwine, we need to tease them apart for this discussion.

Does your child's language level match the nature of the assigned task? Although the connection between language development and homework may seem tenuous at first, as we explore language development further, we see that it is not only interwoven with academics, it is cognitive bedrock. Any discussion of learning must include this topic.

In kindergarten through second grade, children's language usually expands to incorporate the accurate use of pronouns, regular and irregular plurals, endings of degree (big, bigger, biggest), and verb tense endings (jump, jump*s*, jump*ing*, or jump*ed*). Knowing this, you can monitor whether your child is on target, and you can play with the language if your child needs a boost.

It is also during these years that language establishes the vital boundary between reality and fantasy. This development, essential to intellectual and social/emotional growth, depends on language. If your child is still confused, use language and play to help him make this distinction. For example, "Oh, here's a toy mouse. I think I'll lend him my car." Is this real or make believe? Television, with its instant replays, talking tea kettles, real-seeming commercials, and resurrected corpses, complicates your child's task enormously. Use language to help him sort out the differences between virtual and actual.

Language is made of two strands: *receptive* (what the person takes in) and *expressive* (what the person gives out). These two reinforce one another as language grows increasingly robust.

As a parent, you can help your child's receptive language level by conversing, singing, reading aloud, and generally creating a rich language environment. Receptive language needs encouragement.

Expressive language grows through opportunity, an audience, and feedback. Expressive language needs exercise.

The gift of enhanced language is one of the most valuable your child can ever receive. It will enrich life, smooth academic pathways, and create sources of endless personal delight. Giving it is free. Do it.

Just as our bodies are made of flesh, fat, muscle, nerves, sinews, tendons, and bones, language (read or spoken) is made of sounds, words, sentences, paragraphs, description, simile, metaphor, figures of speech, jokes, and different genres. Children need exposure to these before being asked to recognize or assimilate them in reading.

Let's say your child is asked to read an Amelia Bedelia story for homework and then invent a new Amelia Bedelia mistake. If your child has played around with the idea that a single word can have multiple meanings (*dust* as a noun, and *dust* as a verb as in the earlier Amelia Bedelia example) the assignment will be a delight. Otherwise, it will be confusing and frustrating. It would be as if you were trying to repeat a joke when you didn't understand the punch line in the first place.

Research confirms the intuitive sense that early word play is vital. Thus, parents and teachers who want children to be later powerful readers will give ample time to rhyming, making up new words, and breaking words apart and reassembling them (an elephant and a hippopotamus can split and recombine to produce two new species: an ele-potamus and a hippo-phant). Young children who play around with language develop the verbal flexibility that leads to later linguistic resilience.

When you as a parent know

As young children move from baseline language skills to increasingly higher levels, it is as though they are climbing a flight of stairs. Their feet start solidly planted on a step, then, in moving to the next step, one foot stays planted and the other travels the riser aiming for the next step. At that time, the person is standing only on one foot, and balance is precarious. If an event such as the birth of a sibling, separation of parents, death of a grandparent (or beloved hamster), or moving to a new town coincides with unsteady balance, the language, being fragile, may weaken. At such times, the child needs to revert to an earlier language level, re-solidify, and begin the climb again. We see (hear!) this when children with fluent, mature speech revert to baby talk.

these simple truths about language, you can understand both why and how to help your child's language to flower. This is, of course, necessary for homework, and for living as well.

13. Do your child's handwriting skills match the assigned tasks?

Yes, handwriting matters even in an era of electronic miracles. Furthermore, most children in late kindergarten and first and second grade are innately fascinated by the prospect of putting words and ideas on paper. They want to understand the process, and they enjoy exercising the power. Encourage your child in this natural inclination so as to build proficiency while the interest is hot.

Starting in kindergarten, your child needs to develop a correct pencil grip. Trying to change a pencil grip in an older child is like trying to whittle down a mountain with an emery board. Kindergarteners can also learn "the school way" to form letters, and the correct orientation of letters to the line. Seize the moment to ingrain the habit at home.

If your child is not receiving this instruction in school, get a book and teach it at home. (My personal favorite is *Recipe for Reading* by Nina Traub). This is a productive place for you as a parent to fill in a gap without stepping on a teacher's toe or turf. Let your child practice with the formation of her name. If your child's teacher is giving formal handwriting instruction, ask to learn the vocabulary of the instructions and the exact methods for making a "b" or an "s." When you and the teacher use the same lingo, your child will (a) believe you and (b) apply energy to the task instead of to translation.

Here's an example of a problem: let's say your child, who loves projects but has a hard time with handwriting, is asked to do a book report. Check with the teacher to see whether your child can make a five-panel storyboard of the book, complete with captions for each section. Or see whether the book report could be in the form of a diorama (made in a shoe box with scenery and people constructed of paper and clay) with an explanatory card stating title, author, main characters, and setting. That's lots of creativity, evidence of comprehension and very little penmanship. And then, by the way, your child needs to get some handwriting help and practice, too.

14. Do your child's study skills and learning styles match the assigned tasks?

For children this age, the list of necessary study skills is fairly short. The point is for you to help your child establish the foundations that will support more complex and varied academic work later. So, begin at the beginning, keep it simple, and aim for success. Following are some ways you can help your child develop basic study skills.

As a parent, you should create a checklist (using pictures as well as words) of your child's homework routines, in the order in which they should be accomplished. There should be a box to check off each item as it is accomplished. (See sample below.)

Run a bunch of these off the copier so there is one for every day. Your child should fill it in as each task is accomplished and clip it to the finished work when all the boxes are checked off.

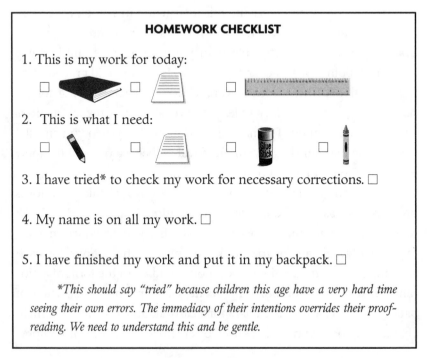

HOMEWORK CHECKLIST

1. This is my work for today:

2. This is what I need:

3. I have tried* to check my work for necessary corrections. ☐

4. My name is on all my work. ☐

5. I have finished my work and put it in my backpack. ☐

   This should say "tried" because children this age have a very hard time seeing their own errors. The immediacy of their intentions overrides their proofreading. We need to understand this and be gentle.

Is this a bit much for little children? If you do it right, it will be a support, not a burden. Do you make a list when you set out to do errands or go marketing? Does it give you a sense of accomplishment (and faith that the ingredients for dinner are captured and stowed) when you have checked everything off? Your child deserves to know how to reach that comfortable state. Children welcome knowing *how*. This shows them.

Knowing how to use a calendar is a vital study skill. Teach your child how to use this helpful tool. Get a big one that shows at least a month at a time. At the end of each day, ask your child to draw a little tiny rebus of something that happened: it rained, Sam threw up, Sally had a birthday, I lost a tooth, Granny came to visit. Look ahead to important events such as holidays and birthdays. Once the calendar has a week or two of notations, your child can go back over the time-line, answering such questions as: "How many days ago was that big rainstorm?" "How many people in our family have birthdays this month?" "Which day of the week is usually your favorite?" Anchoring personal, physical experiences to the abstraction of a chart of white boxes brings the concept of time to life. Your child will come to under-stand the calendar, and people use tools they understand.

For suggestions about the days of the week, months of the year, and the need for analog as well as digital clocks, refer to question 6.

Now is a good time for your child to learn rudimentary skills of summarizing and predicting. People of all ages use these abilities in studying literature or history in school, in setting goals and making business plans in the workplace, and in helping family life move smoothly and joyfully. This is a good use of television. At the end of a program, talk with your child about the most important part of the story. This establishes the concept of finding the main idea, an impor-tant study skill. Play with the title for this same purpose. Ask your child what he would call a particular show if he were going to give it a title, and discuss how you can use a title to decide whether a show sounds appealing. Television, which adults love to hate, can be a useful servant when employed this way.

In addition to these concrete study skills, you need to understand your child's learning styles so you can measure the "goodness of fit" between how your child learns and what she is being asked to do. Just as each person has a unique and permanent fingerprint, each person has an individual learning style.

Learning styles show early, though of course children change and develop new skills as they mature. For this reason, it is silly to say of a six-year-old "Martha is a simultaneous learner." Pigeonholing is dangerous as well as foolish. Your child may show different styles and patterns in different settings and for different requirements. That said, I will also say from experience and from the research that dyslexia, learning disabilities, some kinds of giftedness (academic and other types), and proclivities send up their flags in young children.

Academic giftedness makes children chafe at pedantry, dullness, and repetition. These children need to be able to make connections between what they are learning in school, the outside world, and their imaginations. Potentially, homework is an ideal vehicle. Children who are gifted need time and opportunity to refine their talents as well as to trot in harness with their classmates. Again, homework can be a glorious opportunity.

Dreamers may need to sharpen up. Those who drift may be showing signs of ADD/ADHD (Attention Deficit Disorder/Attention Deficit with Hyperactivity Disorder). These terms are fashionable right now, and may be seriously overused. However, when the condition is real, it is really real. If you suspect this in your child, you may want to consult a neurologist or a psychiatrist.

Some children are both gifted *and* dyslexic or learning disabled. They have particular but manageable needs. Parents and educators need to help them in their areas of need and provide scope and exercise for talents. Unsupported weaknesses ache; unexercised talents itch. Parents need to budget time, money, and psychological and emotional resources accordingly, remembering that "there is life after school," both now and in the long run.

Children who aren't gifted or learning disabled also possess different learning styles. For example, tempo varies widely among little children. Some quick students zoom through concepts and work. Others like to spend lots of time on topics that interest them. Slower children may plod along or, taking only a surface view, skim through and overlook important aspects.

Some learners like to receive small bits of information and then string those together into a concept. They are called *sequential* learners. Others need to see the big overall picture first, then they can break it down into its components, reassembling them into the whole. They are called *simultaneous* learners. In young children, this may show in reading stories. Simultaneous learners may need to see the illustrations first or hear the names of the characters before trying to follow the plot. Trouble follows if a sequential learner has a freewheeling simultaneous teacher or a simultaneous student has a "one foot in front of the other" teacher.

When teaching style and learning style are markedly different, sad to say, the student is usually the one to pay the price. The resulting discomfort can be as intense as that of wearing an unlined jacket of Harris tweed over a new, deep sunburn.

15. What if your child has dyslexia or a learning disability?

Many children who are skillful with their hands and show spatial awareness in their skill on the jungle gym or in assembling puzzles, and who function particularly well in three-dimensional areas, may have weakness on the other side of the coin: the two-dimensional realms such as reading, writing, spelling, and pencil/paper arithmetic. Adults need to be aware of this discrepancy so as to recognize its legitimacy when it appears and then get appropriate help for the child.

Children who have not learned their letters after a teacher has presented the material in such a way that most of the class has caught on should be screened for dyslexia, a condition in which normal to above-average intelligence combines with difficulty learning such arbitrary symbols as letters and sight words. If dyslexia is present, the sooner it is caught the sooner remedies can go to work. Get a tutor if strong, frequent, and consistent help is not available within the school.

Children with diagnosed learning disabilities can learn when taught with appropriate methods and materials. The guiding principle is to break down the tasks into small, manageable bites.

A good resource for information, literature, and conferences is The International Dyslexia Association (I.D.A.), 8600 LaSalle Rd., 382 Chester Building, Baltimore, MD 21286-2044, 410-296-0232.

An attuned parent is the best diagnostician on the planet. If you feel uneasy about your child, if you sense your child is different, if you wake up in the middle of the night with the return of an uneasy feeling, seek professional advice. This will not brand you as a worrywart, you will not be making a problem where none exists, you will not risk labeling your child.

If your child is, in fact, different, if your child is dyslexic, or has trouble with attention, the sooner it's out in the open the better. If the condition remains a private worry, secret fretting will drain your energies. By seeking a diagnosis, you will air the problem. The word may come back that you were right to worry. Fine. Now you can get going with remedies. If the word comes back that everything is normal, you will have disposed of unnecessary emotional baggage.

It's never too early to worry, and it's never too late to help.

16. Are your child's emotional habits and considerations taken into account?

As mentioned in the opening section, Consolidation and Confidence, young children move from learning to love to loving to learn. Consequently, the emotional climate of your child's homework can set the stage for enjoyment and success or for discouragement and self-doubt.

With your help, your child should be encouraged to verbalize his pride or discouragement in what he has done. When he does, you should listen, rephrase, and reinterpret to be sure everyone is on the same page; problem-solve with words; and model constructive behavior.

People of all ages develop emotional habits just as they learn physical habits. Through the experiences you orchestrate and your responses to your child's successes or failures, you play a huge role in the development of optimism and pessimism. Of course, some determination is genetic, but nurture is powerful. Emotional predisposition to optimism or pessimism stacks the deck in favor of success or failure. If there is something your child cannot manage, you can say, "Let's see how we can break this down in little bits, and then we'll be able to do it," or "Let's figure out what was going right and then see what went wrong. That way we can figure it out."

These aren't just "have a nice day" ideas, or things I've thought up on my own. Research and wisdom together show that children flourish when they're encouraged to try new things, make mistakes, and learn from them. From among many leaders in the field of child development, I've chosen three of my favorites to illustrate this point.

Erik Erikson, revered figure in the fields of psychoanalysis and human development, said that school-age children internalize the generalization, "I am what I can make work." Young children equate their worthiness (of parental love) with how they view themselves as students. Adults need to give them things they can "make work." The comments and suggestions about homework you will find in this book speak directly to this issue.

Martin E.P. Seligman, author and professor of psychology at the University of Pennsylvania, demonstrates that children develop feelings of "learned helplessness" or "learned competence" depending on the outcome of their attempts. Those individuals who tend to feel learned helplessness cave in at the prospect of new or hard things and give up quickly in the face of discouragement. Those inclined to feel learned competence tackle challenges with gusto as though sipping from internal wells of Gatorade. The twenty questions we are posing and addressing go a long way towards supplying that Gatorade.

Anthony Bashir, a Boston-based teacher and expert on children's use of language, has said, "We become the story of who we tell ourselves we are."

I saw this myself. One day in school I sought out a first-grader, a boy I knew was having great difficulty with reading. A highly intelligent and wryly humorous boy, he was always fun to talk to and I wanted to take his emotional temperature at the end of his long academic morning. I sat down at his lunch table.

"Hi," I said.

"Hi," he replied, "My name is Alexander."

"Well I know that, Alexander. You're my friend."

"Well," he replied, "you might know that my name is Alexander, but I bet you don't know what it means."

"No, come to think of it, I don't think I do."

With that, this small boy who had struggled so hard, puffed out his chest, squared his shoulders, raised his chin, and looked me directly in the eye.

He said in a low, solemn voice, "It means brave chief and defender of humankind. And that's true," he continued. "You know how I know? My parents tell it to me all the time."

We become the story of who we tell ourselves we are.

My own work has led me into the neuropsychological research on the limbic system, the emotional brain. This particular "mission control" has the power either to open or to close doorways and pathways to learning and memory. Frightened, embarrassed, humiliated, or ashamed kids don't learn new information well. They also lose access to facts and information they already know.

The emotional climate of the home and the classroom is entirely in the hands of parents and teachers. Maintaining an atmosphere of trust, in which it is permissible to take a chance on an idea without fear of ridicule and with tolerance for error, is one of the most sacred trusts adults have. For kindergarten through second grade, the payoff of homework should be consolidation of skills and increased feelings of competence and success. Your priorities as a parent can reinforce or weaken these emotional stances and academic foundations.

17. Does your child's memory capacity match the expectations of the homework?

Memory's four main jobs are to:

- get things in

- file things efficiently and accurately

- retrieve things efficiently and accurately

- use memories in combination with new things to make novel connections

Children in kindergarten through second grade do this unconsciously all day long. So do you. Let's consider two different varieties of memory, and then explore what you can do to help your child build memory skills.

Short-term memory is just what the name implies. Healthy people can remember what they did this morning or an hour ago. Activities and intelligible information go into memory and stick for a short while. During this time, they are available for retrieval and for use.

Long-term memory is also what the name implies. Our minds and our brains transfer some items into long-term storage where they are available for retrieval, now and for decades to come. For example, I visited an Alzheimer's patient today. This man in his eighties is unable to remember the name of the person who has taken care of him for six months, but he can tell you every detail of the winning baseball game he pitched in college.

The trick to storing items in memory lies in moving information from short-term into long-term storage. For instance, in kindergarten through second grade the memory demands on your child might include remembering letter sounds, arithmetic facts, a few pieces of history, sequences in stories, procedural steps for the computer or for following process signs in arithmetic worksheets, what time lunch happens, people's names, and where to line up to get on the right bus to go home.

In order to get these items into storage, people of all ages need to understand what they are doing as they go along. Your child will probably not absorb vocabulary words she doesn't understand, and she cannot "remember" what hasn't gotten in to start with.

How can you help your child? A three-part glue helps things stick:

1) Create a benevolent emotional climate in which intellectual/conceptual risk is safe.

2) Join hands-on physical experience with the event or information.

3) Attach language to the event or information.

As a parent, you can mix up batch after batch of this three-part glue. For example, let's say your child needs to remember the names, housing, crops, and traditions of three Native American Tribes. If your young child sits down and tries to memorize them, she may be successful, or may be successful for a little while but then get muddled.

Here's a way to mix and use the glue: have a snack, a hug, and maybe even turn on some background music. This helps establish a warm emotional climate. Then get three pieces of paper for you and your child to use. With help from you on the spelling (if necessary), have your child write the name of one tribe on the top of each paper. Then, by looking in the book or whatever source material your child has, let her draw and label what people in that tribe used for dwellings. The child who draws and labels a picture of a hogan or pueblo will remember it easily because hands-on activity and information join together on the page. As part three of the glue, continue adding the other bits of information, drawing them, attaching labels, and having discussions until each page is complete. Compare and contrast what each tribe grew, what it would feel like to sleep in the various structures. Bring the illustrations and customs alive through conversation.

Then hang them on the refrigerator and celebrate. When your child takes them into school, the information will be firmly lodged in her memory.

By working on an activity with your child following these (or similar) steps, you enhance the likelihood that your child will store the information in long-term memory.

Some information, such as dates and arithmetic facts, just need to be memorized, and, mercifully, most children this age are good at this rote skill. For such memory demands, remember that three short practices work better than one long one.

Mostly, you and your child need to understand that negative emotions (fear, pessimism, shame), and bodily distress (fatigue, hunger, uncomfortable environments) diminish memory. Positive emotions are enhancers.

18. Does the homework attach new concepts to ones that are already familiar?

Students can't learn two unfamiliars at the same time. They need the "velcro" of the familiar as a place for new information to stick. To acquire new information in an orderly way, people need a supply of general information to act as the familiar onto which to hang what they are learning. A child who has no concept of who Thomas Jefferson was won't hang on to information about Monticello.

For example, if your child shows any confusion with numbers, start with objects. Say to your child, "If I put two cookies here, and add one more, can we count how many cookies there are?" Say the numbers as you touch the objects, and ask your child to do the same. Be sure the child attaches the concept of the number to the object and isn't merely reciting. Normally, children progress from touching objects and moving them around and into new combinations, to drawing pictures of those objects, and then to using numerals to represent those objects. Be sure your child has a solid foundation. Start with objects themselves before moving to the abstraction of numbers.

Make vocabulary familiar through exposure and use, not through teaching lists. For difficult terminology, let the child draw to create context and associations.

And remember that children in these years have huge appetites for new information. By second grade, they are learning the names and distinguishing features of twenty kinds of dinosaurs.

A solid foundation of general knowledge gives new ideas and facts a place to stick. As parents, you can help supply that knowledge and build that foundation in the following four ways:

First, help your child put experiences into words. Language is one ingredient of the memory glue. This is an ideal situation for introducing new vocabulary and attaching it to the child's actual experiences.

Second, discuss current events—elections, sports, local events, and national figures—so that these names and concepts are part of your child's conceptual equipment.

Third, use television as one of many sources of information on current events, thus providing food for thought and discussion. As mentioned in the discussion of question 14, television, used wisely, can be more than cognitive anesthesia.

Fourth, tell family stories. Be specific about where and when they happened, what life was like at that time. My grandchildren like to hear about my mother, a diminutive beauty born in 1898, who wore hats with veils and smoked Parliament cigarettes in long white holders. She carried a fur muff and went sledding in high-heeled boots.

In addition to being fun and weaving a rich tapestry of personal family associations, family stories provide historical context, vocabulary, imagery, emotional identification . . . all of which are the foundations of understanding literature and identifying with various eras in history.

19. Does your child's homework promote privacy, participation, and enjoying your kid?

Privacy. Young children need privacy as they make the errors that accompany all learning. Kids don't really like to make mistakes in front of the people they want to please—like you. This does not imply that mistakes are shameful. You can underscore this message. And remember that you give a gift of trust when you allow your child privacy.

Participation gives your child a chance to share as much as he wants about a current project or reading level, and gives you a chance to delight in burgeoning accomplishments without being nosy.

Perhaps the most important charter you have as a parent is to get a kick out of your child. Hard to codify yet unmistakably easy to recognize, this is a vote of confidence which, in turn, inspires confidence. If you enjoy your child's independent accomplishments, the child will feel proud and valued. If you hang the chart of Native American Tribes on the refrigerator or help your child send it along to a distant grandparent, the contagion of your enjoyment will warm your child's heart.

20. Do you watch the Plimsoll Line?

"The Plimsoll Line (sometimes called the Plimsoll Mark) is a circle with a horizontal line drawn through it, carried on both sides of all British merchant vessels. It indicates the maximum depth to which a vessel may be loaded, and is named after Samuel Plimsoll (1824-98) . . . who brought about its adoption in view of the great loss of life in overloaded vessels."

—*Brewer's Dictionary of Phrase and Fable*

 Try to imagine your child as a boat with a hull, captain, crew, cargo, home port, and destination. The goal should be buoyancy, safety, and a successful journey. You, ideally in cooperation with teachers, need to watch your child's Plimsoll Line.

If you as a parent have a respect for learning, an enjoyment of what your child can accomplish independently, a willingness to tackle new learning yourself, a confidence in the priorities you have built into the intimate fabric of your family life, and a willingness to share troubles as well as triumphs with the educators who are with your child every day, you will communicate these priorities, reinforce intellectual and emotional strengths, and help your child chart an individual course to vigor and enjoyment.

Bon voyage!

Priscilla L. Vail, M.A.T.

For more books and materials by Priscilla L. Vail, visit:
http://www.priscillavail.com

CHAPTER 1

Developing Good Homework Habits

THE TIME AND SPACE HOMEWORK PACT—a "contract" between you and your child regarding where and when homework will be completed (see Introduction)—is the foundation on which success in schoolwork rests.

This chapter will discuss all the various details—such as location and materials—necessary to make the Homework Pact effective. These details are like the fine print of a contract. However, before we get to all the small points, let's take a look at the Big Picture.

A *good homework location should have adequate lighting as well as an area of flat space where your child can lay out some books and paper.*

Location, Location, Location

As previously discussed in the Introduction, a good spot to do homework is one where your child can work without any major distractions. After you agree upon a location where your child will work, give him the opportunity to decorate it with posters, a corkboard with pictures of his friends, or other items that make him feel comfortable, but will not distract him from his homework for a long period of time.

Tools of the Trade

Following are a list of supplies that are helpful to have available in the homework location:

ESSENTIAL SCHOOL ITEMS

Pencils

Eraser

Crayons or markers

Paper, lined and unlined. (The lined paper is helpful for penmanship exercises.)

Ruler

Dictionary (A children's dictionary is preferable.)

Notebooks

*T*o compute or not to compute? Computer access at home is a nice convenience, but your child's education will not suffer if you don't own one. While students are often taught to use computers in school, there are no homework assignments that require your child to own a home computer. If your child needs access to a computer, many schools and local libraries have computer labs.

Keep in mind that computers can also be a source of distraction. If your child has access to the Internet, she can easily spend several hours on the Web surfing instead of working. You may even want to check in on her occasionally to make sure that there is actual education afoot, and not some fast and furious video game.

NON-ESSENTIAL BUT HELPFUL ITEMS

Glue

Scissors (Safety scissors, of course.)

Posterboard

A sheaf of colored papers

USEFUL REFERENCE ITEMS

None of these items is crucial to any assignment your child will face, but having them around can prove beneficial.

Thesaurus

Grammar book

Encyclopedia (CD-ROM version or regular)

Atlas

Certain projects may require additional supplies, which you can purchase on a case-by-case basis.

The supplies listed are definitely useful items to have around, but don't tear your hair out if you don't have them. While it would be great to have access to an encyclopedia at your house, your child can get by just as easily by using the encyclopedias at the nearest branch library, or the ones at the school library, for that matter.

How To Help Your Child With Cold, Hard Facts

Often your child's homework assignments will involve quests for facts. A good approach for this kind of assignment is to set up a series of steps your child should follow before asking for help from you. For example, you might try the following technique:

First, your child should give every question his best shot, skipping over problems that are giving him trouble during his first pass through. Then, he should spend some additional time trying to figure out the tough problems on his own, turning to other resources if necessary. If the extra time and other resources don't help, it's your turn to step in. When you do, remember:

•••••

Telling your child the right answer to a question is not as helpful as teaching him how to find the right answer to a question.

•••••

So if your child asks you where the Rocky Mountains are located, try saying something like, "Let's think about it this way: what reference material could we use to find the answer to this question?" If your child says "dictionary," help him check the dictionary. It turns out many dictionaries do list major mountain ranges, bodies of water, deserts, and so forth. If your child says "globe," "map," "atlas," or "encyclopedia," a quick survey of the proper map or atlas page would also yield the correct answer. Using this method, your child learns not only that the Rocky Mountains extend from central New Mexico to northern Alaska, but also that this type of information can be found in an atlas, dictionary, or globe. This way, your child learns—and learns how to learn more in the future.

Another way to help your child on fact-based homework assignments is to encourage the use of **mnemonic** (pronounced "nuh-mon-ick") **devices**. Although a mnemonic device sounds like an expensive electronic gadget, it is in fact just a tool to help your child remember a certain fact. For example, let's say your child's assignment was to look up twenty vocabulary words and write down their definitions. This is a straightforward assignment, but the key is to *understand the goal of the homework assignment.* In this case the goal is to learn the definitions of the twenty assigned words. If your child just writes down the definitions or doesn't understand a lick of what he's writing, he is going to have trouble when the time comes for him to define the vocabulary words on his own.

Here is where a mnemonic device comes in handy. We can use a word like *squint* as an example. After you tell your child the definition of this word, the two of you can have a "Squint-Down" competition, much like a shootout but much less dangerous. Start with your face in a relaxed normal position. Once one of you says, "Squint!" both sides have to scrunch up their eyes as much as possible. Fastest or goofiest-looking squint wins. Once your child has a couple of rounds of Squint-Down under his belt, remembering the word will be easier. The dictionary definition of squint is "to look with eyes partly closed," and this describes exactly what you do to your face during a round of Squint-Down. Instead of trying to remember a dry dictionary definition, your child can use the mnemonic device of this game to remember the word's meaning. This is much easier to remember, and when the time comes to define *squint* on a test, your child should be able to give its meaning.

Not every word or fact lends itself to a mnemonic device. Some things will just have to be memorized (this is especially true of the spelling of many English words). However, if you encourage your child to come up with mnemonic devices, it should help improve his memory, and it will make basic homework assignments designed to increase your child's base of knowledge more effective.

How to Help with Creative Projects

You might not think that building a diorama of the prehistoric era or drawing a poster illustrating a favorite multicultural event requires help, but even children in the early grade levels benefit from solid planning techniques. Sit down with your child before the project begins and help her plan out the various steps needed to complete her assignment. You'll both benefit by eliminating late nights, tears, or projects that have to be discarded because a crucial element was left out. Here are some questions you should ask your child.

In the most detailed terms possible, what do you want the final project to be?

Ask your child questions to help her turn a broad idea, "My poster will have something to do with sports," into a specific idea, "My poster will show my favorite part of four sports: heading a soccer ball, making a lay-up, spiking the volleyball, and diving off the high dive."

What steps do you need to take to complete the assignment?

This question helps your child break a large project into a series of manageable tasks so that she doesn't get overwhelmed. Does your child want to draw the poster in pencil first and then color it in? Does she want to cut out pictures from magazines and paste them onto the poster? Try asking, "How will you fill the space on the page?" This question will decrease the likelihood that your child will draw a tiny picture on a huge piece of paper or draw an object too large for the piece of paper.

What materials do you need for your project?

Once your child has laid out all the various steps, she needs to decide what tools and supplies she will need to accomplish each stage of the project. Is she going to use crayons or markers for her poster? Does she have posterboard? Will she need scissors or glue? Magazines or newspapers? Does she want to cut everything out first, and then do all of the pasting?

Roughly how long will each step of the project take?

Since children this age are still developing a concept of time, you'll need to help your child figure out if the tasks she's described are too involved for the amount of time she has to complete the project. If she wants to paint her sports poster and then glue on pictures from a magazine, but she only has an hour before her bedtime, you might need to step in and suggest cutting out all of the pictures before bed, and then getting up a little bit early in the morning to do the pasting.

We're not saying that a poster, card, or diorama needs to be planned out as strategically as a political campaign; rather, the goal here is simply to discuss these questions with your child in a casual, interested manner when she describes the project.

What if You Get Stumped by Your Child's Homework?

While this might not happen at the primary school level, it is bound to happen one day. Your child will ask you a question or show you a homework problem that you can't even *understand,* much less answer. The main reason for this is that the terms you used in school are not always the same ones your child is learning. For example, you wouldn't think a word like *subtract* would ever go out of style, but in some areas this word has been replaced by synonyms like *reduce* or *lessen.*

When faced with the inevitable stumper, don't worry. Remember, you may have forgotten a few things, but you are still much more experienced than your child at finding the information that you need. You can turn the occasion into a learning experience for both you and your child as you track down the answer together.

If your child asks you a question with an unfamiliar phrase, ask her if you can see an example of the phrase. It might be on a handout, or in a book of some sort. Many times, when you see an example, you will understand the meaning of the new term.

Can You Make Doing Homework an Enjoyable Experience?

*C*hildren who are just starting school often enjoy the responsibility of homework—they get to do work just like the big kids do. Yet when a new or difficult concept arises, very young kids often feel more overwhelmed than older children because *learning* is still new to them. You can help transform homework into something your child does not fear, just something that needs to be done to learn the material. Remember, your attitude about homework has a big impact on your child's attitude about homework. Your child will probably have initial trouble with some topics, but he can learn the material well with your help. Homework is not always an enjoyable experience: sometimes the gratification has to wait until your child takes a test on that subject . . . and aces it.

This is when you'll both feel like Homework Heroes.

CHAPTER 2

A Review of Basic K-2
Math Concepts

FOLLOWING IS A REVIEW OF the four major concepts that are the linchpins of math at this level: Number Sense, Geometry and Measurement, Algebra (yes, believe it or not, your first-grader may learn basic algebra), and Computation and Analysis. You will be familiar with most of these topics, but you might have forgotten some of the terminology involved. If you refamiliarize yourself with these ideas and terms, you should have the foundation you need to help with any math homework at the kindergarten through second-grade level.

Number Sense

Key Idea: Whole Numbers

At the kindergarten level, the first goal will be for your child to learn the numbers from 0 to 10. Simple counting questions, such as, "What number comes after 4?" or "List all the whole numbers between 6 and 9," are good primers for this concept. The phrase *whole numbers* is used because there are, in fact, an infinite amount of numbers between 6 and 9—for example, there's 6.01, 6 ½, and 6.00000347 to name just three. A **whole number**, however, is a number that has no fractions or decimals; so the correct answer to the question, "List all the whole numbers between 6 and 9," would be, "7 and 8."

Although negative numbers are too advanced for the earliest grade levels, you should know that whole numbers can be negative numbers, too. So -6 and 6 are both whole numbers.

A good way to illustrate the concept of whole numbers is to use a **number line**, like the one below.

```
0   1   2   3   4   5   6   7   8   9   10
```

Ask your child to look at the space between 0 and 1 on the number line. That's where all numbers greater than zero, but less than 1, can be found. This includes simple fractions like ½ and ¼, which your child will be exposed to by second grade. All the numbers with dash marks above them are the whole numbers. Have your child place one finger on the 6 and another on the 9—she should now be able to see that 7 and 8 are the only whole numbers between 6 and 9.

Key Idea: Greater Than, Less Than, and Equal To

The equal sign, = , is the most common of the three terms listed above, and it is used to show that two sides of an equation have the same value. Examples include 4 = 4, or 2 + 6 = 5 + 3. Your child will see many equations with one side missing, such as the problem below.

EXAMPLE:

2 + 1 + 3 =

In essence, this addition problem asks your child to fill in the right side of the equation with a number that is equal to the left side of the equation. The correct answer to this problem would be 6,since

2 + 1 + 3 = 6

This is the answer her teacher is probably looking for. Still, to reinforce the concept of equality, you could show your child that

2 + 1 + 3 = 1 + 1 + 1 + 1 + 1 + 1 and 2 + 1 + 3 = 5 + 1

Both of these equations are also correct answers to the original equation above, since the two sides of each equation equal 6.

While the equal sign looks like =, the *greater than* sign looks like > and the less than symbol looks like <. The greater than and less than symbols seem interchangeable, since 6 < 9 and 9 > 6 are both true, but the first expression means that 6 *is less than* 9 and the second one says that 9 *is greater than* 6. If your child is easily confused by these symbols, tell him to remember this:

• • • • •

On less than/greater than problems, always think of greedy crocodiles.

• • • • •

You see, the < and > symbols are actually the jaws of a crocodile. All crocodiles are greedy, and they always like to eat the largest amount (number) possible. Therefore, the jaws of the crocodile always look as if they are about to eat the biggest number.

EXAMPLE:

Fill in the blanks below with the proper symbol.

4 __ 7　　　　　3 + 1 __ 9 − 8　　　　　4 + 0 __ 2 + 2

Number lines can help your child understand a variety of math concepts, including greater than, less than, and equal to. Use the number line on page 44 and have your child place his hands on both the four and the seven. The number that is closer to zero is the smaller number, or you could say the number farther from zero is the greater number, which means the same thing.

In the first example, the crocodile is definitely going to eat the 7, since it's larger, so 4 < 7. Since the < is used, the proper way to say this is "four is less than 7." In the second example, the first equation equals 4, and the second equation equals 1. The proper symbol, therefore, is >, and the expression is stated as "4 is greater than 1." The last expression is equal, so it gets an equal sign.

Key Idea: Counting

Learning the names of the numbers from 1 through 100 is something your child will focus on in kindergarten, or first grade at the latest. At first, this might consist of learning smaller subsets—the first twenty numbers to start, then 1 through 50—before tackling the entire range from 1 through 100.

Learning these numbers is primarily a memorization skill, so you can help by quizzing your child during the course of the day. For example, if your child wants to play at a neighbor's house, you can say, "You can go after you recite all the numbers from 1 to 40." Kids love a good challenge, and your child will probably speed through them as fast as possible. Correct her if she makes any errors, and help her if she gets stuck for too long, because you don't want this memory drill to become too difficult.

It is important to get your child comfortable with manipulating numbers in a variety of ways. Really, counting backwards is nothing more than a subtraction drill. Giving your child a firm foundation in basic math skills is the major aspect of almost all kindergarten through second grade math homework.

Key Idea: Place Value

Most adults can look at the number 6,423 and know exactly what that means, but you might have a harder time if someone asked you for the "units digit" of 6,423. This is a case of primary school terminology that has been left way back in the dusty corner of our minds.

In order to find the units digit, your child must first understand place values. The numbers from one to nine have one digit each; numbers from 10 to 99 have two digits. For example, the number 10 has a 1 and a 0. The "0" in the number 10 is in the **units** place (this is also called the **ones** place), and it means there are no 1s. (In the number 16, the "6" means there are six 1s.) The "1" is in the **tens** place, which means that there is one group of 10. The "2" in 20 stands for two groups of 10, and so on. Numbers from 100 to 999 also have a **hundreds** place, so in the number 500, the "5" stands for five groups of 100. Now, going back to the example on the previous page, your child should be able to tell you that the units digit is 3.

There are two main homework questions that revolve around number terminology. The first is like the question above, which asks your child what value each digit in a number represents.

EXAMPLE:

In the number 8,916, the number 9 is in the _____ place.

A. units

B. tens

C. hundreds

D. thousands

The number 9 is in the hundreds place.

A similar question type asks your child to change a number into a word. Technically, this could be called switching from the numeric system (1-9) to the alphabetic system (A-Z). Still, you should not get technical with your child, so "switching from numbers to letters" is the best way to talk about it with your kid.

To switch from numbers to letters, we will continue to use the units-tens-hundreds terminology. Look at 8,916 again. We know that the 8 is in the thousands place, 9 is in the hundreds place, 1 is the tens place, and 6 is the units digit. To write out this number then, we would say:

Eight thousand, nine hundred sixteen = 8,916.

When children write a number, or speak a number out loud, they have a tendency to add the word *and* to the number, such as "Nine thousand and eight hundred and sixteen." While this is not harmful in any way, it is not the proper way to pronounce the number. Gently encourage your child to leave out the word *and* when writing out or speaking a number. This rule is like some of the finer points of grammar: some teachers will let it slide but others won't, so it's best to be prepared for the toughest scenario.

You will notice that the written number doesn't say "eight-thousand, nine hundred, ten and six units." This is because the numbers 1 through 99 have their own particular way of being spoken, which is why counting is a key idea in these early years.

EXAMPLE:

Write out the numeric value of two-thousand six.

Here's a tough question, not for what it contains, but for what it does not. If your child had this as a homework problem, the best approach would be to ask your child leading questions to help him through his place value terminology. For example, you might ask, "What is the value of the thousands digit?" or "What is the value of the hundreds digit?" The only values given are for the thousands place (2) and the units place (6), but if he understands the progression of thousands-hundreds-tens-units, then he will know that in between the 2 in the thousands place and the 6 in the units place, he needs to fill in the hundreds and tens values. Since no value is given, a zero must hold that value's place in each case, so the answer to the question is 2,006.

Key Idea: Ordinals

You might be unfamiliar with the word *ordinal*, but you probably know the concept. Ordinal numbers are numbers that show place or position within a sequence, such as *first, second,* and *third.* Homework assignments about ordinal numbers will test your child's ability to understand the idea of sequence. Sometimes kids get tripped up on ordinals because they're confused by the fact that the number 10 is greater (larger) than the number 1, yet it's better to be in first place than tenth place. Just explain to your child that when it comes to ordinals, less (smaller) is better. Then point out that if she's tenth on line at her favorite ice cream parlor, she has to wait for nine other people to get served before she does; if she's first on line, there are zero people ahead of her and she should place her order! This should clear things up pretty quickly.

EXAMPLE:

Betty was at the head of the line for tickets. Jerry and Mike were right behind her, and Santos was right behind them. Complete the following sentence correctly: Santos was in _____ place on line.

All the counting drills your child did may help her on this problem. You can answer the question by counting in ascending order by ones, but you have to use ordinal numbers. Your child might want to create a list similar to this one:

First	Betty
Second	Jerry (or Mike)
Third	Mike (or Jerry)
Fourth	Santos
Fifth	...
Sixth	...

Santos was in fourth place.

Key Idea: Addition/Subtraction

The concepts of addition (putting two numbers together) and subtraction (taking a number away from another number) are something your child should be able to understand fairly easily. If he does not, just take away his favorite toy: that's subtraction for you. (We're kidding!) A gentler way of teaching subtraction would be to take away the food at dinner that he doesn't like. This will not only help him understand subtraction, but actually enjoy it.

There are different levels of addition and subtraction. Some of the many steps have been listed below, starting with the least difficult before moving onto harder concepts.

Simple single-digit addition/subtraction

This is the "Fingers and Toes" stage, and it really is fine if your child uses his fingers (and toes) to help him out. He will also learn that an addition sign looks like +, and a subtraction sign looks like −. These questions consist of adding one number from 1 to 9 to another number from 1 to 9, or subtracting one single-digit number from another. If your child is having trouble with single-digit problems, use objects from around the house or draw pictures to help him attach the concept of the number to the objects in front of him (sweets and comic books are always popular objects). You can also practice manipulating these objects, adding and subtracting some from the pile and seeing if your child can figure out the new number that's represented.

Filling in or completing a pattern

If you did counting drills (page 47) with your child, then she already has some experience with this level. If your child is given the pattern "3, 6, 9, 12, ___" and asked what number comes next, your child will have to add 3 to the last number to get the correct answer. Essentially, then, you're solving the problem, "What does 12 + 3 equal?"

Some toys are tailor-made for mathematic manipulation. A set of simple wooden blocks can provide a great deal of math practice for your child. For simple addition, you can build towers of blocks, counting upwards as you go. The subtraction part of this game is more fun for your child, as he gets to smash down the blocks and then count how many are left standing. Once the blocks are on the ground, your child can count the ones remaining and do a little subtraction to figure out how many blocks must be scattered on the ground.

Other household items, such as straws or cotton balls, can also be fashioned into interesting math manipulating games.

Adding/Subtracting two double-digit numbers

This level can be broken into two categories of its own: *with regrouping* and *without regrouping.*

*T*he first step your child should take when adding or subtracting multiple-digit numbers is to write the numbers in columns and make sure the place values match up (units lined up with units, tens with tens, and so forth). If he doesn't, this means he is trying to answer the problem in his head, and that can lead to mental mistakes. Therefore, take something like

22 + 30 + 8 + 14 = ___ and make sure to write it out

```
 22
 30
  8
+14
```

Notice that the 8 is aligned with the other units digits, not the tens.

Then, your child can proceed accordingly.

Addition

For addition, regrouping means your child has to "carry" a tens digit. For example,

---
EXAMPLE:

23	23
+15	+49

In the first problem, no regrouping is needed. You simply add the units digits together, 3+5, and get 8. Then add the tens digits together, 2 + 1, to get 3. The correct answer is 38.

In the second problem, regrouping is needed, because when the units digits are added together, 3 + 9, the answer is 12, so you need to write down the 2 in the units column and carry the tens digit, 1, over to the left. When adding the tens digits together, it now becomes 2 + 4 + 1 = 7, so the final answer is 72.

Forgetting to carry the 1 is a very common mistake young students make. By not regrouping, they end up with 62 as the answer.

Subtraction

With subtraction, regrouping takes a similar form, although instead of carrying the number over from the units to the tens place, you have to "borrow" from the tens to give to the units.

EXAMPLE:

$$63 \qquad\qquad 75$$
$$-\ \underline{12} \qquad\qquad -\ \underline{28}$$

On the first problem, you subtract the units digits, $3 - 2$, to get 1. Then subtract the tens digits, $6 - 1 = 5$, so the final answer is 51.

On the second problem, though, subtracting the units is problematic because $5 - 8$ would give you a negative number. To fix this, you have to reduce the tens digit, 7, to 6, and then take that borrowed "1" and give it to the units digits, so that "5" becomes "15."

Written out, it would look like

$$75 \qquad\qquad \overset{6\ \ 15}{\cancel{75}}$$
$$-\ \underline{28} \qquad\qquad -\ \underline{28}$$

This way, the first step of subtraction is now $15 - 8$, which equals 7. The next step is to subtract the tens digits, $6 - 2$, so that the final answer is 47.

Adding multiple numbers

The chances that regrouping will be needed increases as the quantity of numbers being added together increases. In fact, if enough numbers are strung together, your child might have to carry a tens digit larger than "1".

> **O**ne way to explain this regrouping movement to your child is to have him think about the number 75 as seven groups of 10 and five 1s. If you take away one of the 10s and add it to the group of five 1s, what do you get? The answer is "fifteen," so now, instead of 75 being seven 10s and five 1s, it has been shuffled around into six 10s and fifteen. Numerically, this looks like $70 + 5 = 60 + 15$.

EXAMPLE:

$$32 \qquad\qquad 19$$
$$46 \qquad\qquad 38$$
$$\underline{+\ 7} \qquad\qquad \underline{+\ 6}$$

In the first example, you could add two of the numbers in the units column together, get the sum, and then add the third units digits to that number. Of course, you can add all three of them together at the same time, but your child should understand the easiest method first before jumping into the more advanced approach. Therefore, start by adding 2 + 6, which equals 8, and then add 8 to the 7 that remains. 8 + 7 = 15, so write down the 5 and carry the "1" over to the tens column. You now have 1 + 3 + 4 = 8. Again, you can break this down by first adding 1 + 3 to get 4, and then adding the remaining 4 to that; either way, you get 8, so the final answer is 85.

In the second example, add the units digits from the first two numbers, 9 + 8 = 17. When you then add the last number, 6, to the units part, you gets 17 + 6 = 23. Therefore, you must write down the 3 in the units column and "carry" the 2 over to the tens column. Adding all the numbers in the tens column now becomes 2 (carried over) + 1 + 3 = 6, so the answer is 63.

Subtracting multiple numbers is a subject too difficult for most beginning students, so it's doubtful your child will encounter it in a homework assignment. If he does, the key is to remember that only two numbers can be subtracted at any one time (a larger number from a smaller number). So in the problem 54 – 13 – 34, first tackle 54 – 13, and then take that answer (41) and subtract 34 from it, 41 – 34 = 7.

Counting coins/Simple word problems

This type of problem is more advanced than the others, because your child will have to decide first what the problem should look like, and then perform the math correctly. It is the difference between the following two questions:

EXAMPLE A:

25
10
10
+5

EXAMPLE B:

Jonathan has a quarter, two dimes, and a nickel in his piggy bank. How much money does Jonathan have in his piggy bank?

Both questions have the same answer, but the second question is more difficult because your child must first set up the problem correctly. You can help your child think through the steps involved by asking questions like, "How many coins does Jonathan have in his bank?" There are four in all because of the two dimes. Your next question would be, "How much is a quarter worth?" then "How much is a dime worth?" and "How many dimes does he have?" and so on. In the end, your child should come up with the equation that is shown in Example A. All that remains is to add the numbers correctly, and the answer is 50 cents.

As you can see, many coin problems are simple word problems. Other word problems will talk about other things, such as fruit.

EXAMPLE:

There are fourteen bananas in the fruit bowl. If Jingy the pet monkey eats six of them, how many bananas remain?

Greedy Jingy! To find the answer, your child will first have to realize that this is a subtraction problem. After that, if he sets up the equation properly, $14 - 6 =$ ___, he should be able to solve for the correct answer, 8.

Often, simple word problems will be accompanied by some visual information, such as a drawing of fourteen bananas. If this is the case,

Homework Heroics: Making Change

IF YOU WANT to give your child extra help counting coins, take the coins out of your pocket at the end of each day and ask your child to count them. If you're feeling generous, let him keep the change if he does so correctly.

another way to complete the problem would be the cross out six bananas, and then count the remaining bananas.

You can use these five different levels when helping your child with addition/subtraction homework. If he gets confused on a problem, determine the level of the question, and then go one level easier. Talk about problems at that level, and when your child is comfortable with them, return to the harder problem. This accomplishes some positive things: it helps your child regain his confidence by going over material he understands, and it makes explaining the slightly more difficult question much easier.

Key Idea: Estimation

To estimate means to calculate roughly or approximately. At the kindergarten through second-grade level, estimation will be limited primarily to rounding up or down by 10s. The rules of estimating using this method are fairly straightforward:

ESTIMATING BY UNITS OF 10

**If the units digit is 1, 2, 3, or 4, then you round down to the nearest ten.
14 becomes 10.**

**If the units digit is 6, 7, 8, or 9, then you round up to the nearest ten.
46 becomes 50.**

**If the units digit is 5, then you round down if the tens digit is even, but you round up if the tens digit is odd.
25 becomes 20.
35 becomes 40.**

As you might imagine, it's the last rule that is tricky. In fact, you probably won't see it too much at this level. If your child is having trouble with estimating, have her draw a number line. This visual representation will help her understand to which multiple of 10 she should round the number.

Advanced Number Sense Concepts

The following concepts might be introduced at the second-grade level, so we're discussing them here briefly; however, these are advanced topics, so there's no need to be worried if your child's homework does not contain these concepts.

Advanced Key Idea: Adding and Subtracting Three-digit Numbers

Addition and subtraction become a little trickier when you add another digit, simply because there will be more regrouping. A homework question might look like

---

EXAMPLE:

$$345$$
$$+789$$

This problem isn't necessarily more complex, there's just more of it now. Instead of regrouping once, your child will now have to regroup twice. Adding the units digits, 5 + 9, makes 14, so the 4 remains and the "1" is carried over to the tens column. There you have 1 + 4 + 8 = 13, so the 3 remains and the new "1" is carried to the hundreds column. In the hundreds column, you now have 1 + 3 + 7 = 11. If there were more digits, you would have to carry again, but there aren't, so the final answer is 1,134.

Explain to your child that the only difference between two-digit addition and three-digit addition is that there are more computations to make, and that means there's a greater chance of making a careless error. However, if he writes his work out neatly and makes sure to carry numbers correctly, then it won't mater if he's adding a nine-digit number with another nine-digit number—he should still be able to solve the problem correctly.

Advanced Key Idea: Understanding and Comparing Fractions

Only the simplest fractions will be covered at the kindergarten through second-grade level, often in pictorial form. Consider the following hypothetical homework problem.

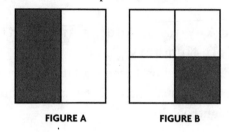

FIGURE A   FIGURE B

EXAMPLE:

Which Figure is half-shaded, and which Figure is ¼ shaded?
Which fraction is greater, ½ or ¼ ?

A fraction represents a part of a whole. The top number in the fraction is the "part," or numerator, and the bottom number is the "whole," or denominator. Figure A is made up of two parts, but only one box is shaded, so the fraction of Figure A that is shaded is ½.

Fraction   = Part/whole
= number of shaded boxes/total number of boxes
= ½

The number line is another good way to explain fractions. Explain to your child that the numbers between different whole numbers are fractions. It helps to draw a number line with a large space between 0 and 1, and focus on the fractions that exist between those two numbers.

In Figure B, the "whole" is made up of four different boxes, so the bottom number of the fraction is 4. Only one box, or "part" is shaded, so the top number in the fraction is 1, which gives us the fraction ¼.

The second question in this problem, "Which fraction is greater?" can be answered visually, by looking at the two figures. Both figures are the same size, and the shaded part of Figure A is obviously larger, so the answer must be ½. Having the picture is an important part of this question, since many students would pick ¼ over ½ without the visual assistance. In their minds, since 4 is greater than 2, ¼ must be larger than ½. Keep this in mind if your child has homework problems that ask her to compare fractions without any illustrations. Simply drawing out a figure with the proper part/whole ratio is an excellent way to help your child understand the concept of fractions.

Advanced Key Idea: Simple Multiplication and Division

In the second grade, multiplication and division usually deal with

---

Homework Heroics: Multiplication and Division Baseball

HERE'S A GREAT way to help your child practice simple multiplication and division.

The Official Rules of Multiplication and Division Baseball

1) Get four paper plates and place them on the floor in a diamond pattern. Label the bases Home, First, Second, and Third.

2) Your child steps up to home plate. You, the pitcher, lob a multiplication question at him, such as "What is 4 times 8?" Your child only has a small amount of time—you decide the length—to hit back with the correct answer. If he does, he gets to advance to first base. An incorrect answer, or no answer at all, results in an out. After three outs, the inning is over.

3) If more than one child is playing, it is now their turn to step up to the plate and answer a question. If it's only you and your child, it's time to employ the ever-popular Ghost Runner on first. Your child returns to the plate, and if he gets another question right, the Ghost Runner on first moves to second, and so forth.

Play can continue for as many innings as you like. If there's only one child playing, you can set a run-scoring goal, such as 10 runs in a three-inning game.

Play Ball!

---

numbers in the 0 to 100 range, so 10 multiplied by (or "times") 10 is likely the most difficult problem your child will encounter. Learning simple multiplication and division, such as 2×3 or $4 \div 2$, is often just a straight memorization drill. Your child is given a Multiplication or Division Table, and asked to memorize it.

If this is the case, one way to help your child is to use the memorization drilling ideas discussed on page 46 as a way to quiz your child on the facts. Flashcards are also very helpful when learning multiplication and division.

Those are the basic Number Sense ideas your child will experience. It's now time to shift gears a bit, and start discussing

Geometry and Measurement

Geometry

There will be very little abstract geometry at this point in your child's education. Instead, geometry assignments will focus on teaching your child to recognize several basic geometric shapes. She won't have to know the precise mathematical definitions for them; she just has to be able to differentiate a triangle from a square.

The following pages illustrate the most common **planar** (two-dimensional) and **solid** (three-dimensional) shapes, and provide some basic characteristics of each.

Key Idea: Gallery of Most Wanted Geometric Shapes

All agents beware: These shapes are usually friendly, but can be dangerous when swallowed or stacked too high. Stay on the lookout for these shapes during your daily routine, and you'll see them everywhere: as traffic signs, billboards, mailboxes, ice cream cones, and other everyday objects.

Planar Shapes
Name: Circle

Also known as: Ring, Halo, and Loop

CIRCLE

Description: The circle is a tricky customer to catch, mainly because it has no corners. The outside is a continuous curved line. The center of the circle is the same distance from every point along its edge. This is how a circle is different from an oval, which often looks like a circle stretched on one or more sides.

Name: Oval

Also known as: Ellipse

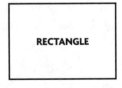

Description: An oval is similar to a circle since it has no corners, only a continuous curved edge. However, unlike a circle, if you were to place a point in the middle of an oval, not every point on the edge would be the same distance from it. An oval looks like an egg.

Name: Square

Description: The square is a shape with four sides and four corners. All four sides have the same length. The four corners meet at right angles, which means the angles are 90 degrees.

Name: Rectangle

Description: Just as the oval is the stretched-out cousin of the circle, the rectangle is a Silly-Putty'd version of the square. The rectangle has four sides, and four corners that all meet in right angles. However, unlike the square, not all sides are of equal length: its opposite sides are of equal length and parallel to each other. Normally, the longer side is called the *length,* while the shorter side is the *width.*

A 90-degree angle is also called a right angle. Spare your child the mathematical proof and just show her examples of right angles until she can recognize them. Have her hold out one hand, with her palm forward. Keep the finger straight, and gently pull the thumb as far away as possible. The angle formed by the thumb and the index finger is approximately a right angle (although it's a gentle one because of the skin). Your child will see that the angles in the triangle below are not right angles.

Name: Diamond

Also known as: Rhombus

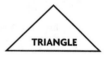

Description: A diamond is like a square that got a little tired and bent over. It is a four-sided figure, and each side is the same length as the others (and its opposite sides are parallel). However, none of the four corners of a rhombus are right angles.

Name: Triangle

Description: A triangle is a figure with three sides and three angles. These sides can be a variety of different lengths, just so long as all three are connected to form a figure. The three inside angles can vary greatly as well.

Solid Shapes

Most planar shapes have two-dimensions: they have *length* and *width*. Solid shapes have three-dimensions, since they add the dimension *height*. As your child can see, many solid shapes are very similar to their planar relatives. The best example of this is the cube and the square, since a cube is a square with an added dimension—height—tacked onto it.

Name: Cube

Description: There are six squares on every cube, and these six sides are called the *faces* of a cube. A cube, then, is a solid with six equal, square faces. Every *edge* of a cube is the same length (your child should be able to see how the sides of each square now form the edges of the cube.) Also, the interior angles of a cube are all right angles.

Name: Box

Description: The box is simply a rectangle with height added to it. It is different from a cube because not all the *faces* are the same size; on a box, opposite faces are of equal length and parallel to each other. All of the corners meet at right angles.

Name: Sphere

Also known as: Ball, Globe, Orb

Description: Like the circle, a sphere has no corners, just a continuous curved surface. Remember how each point on the edge of a circle was the same distance from the center of that circle? Well, the same holds true for a sphere, only this time the points along the surface are in three dimensions, not just two.

To show how a sphere is like a circle, imagine cutting a sphere in half. If you looked inside, you would see a circle.

Name: Cone

Description: Your child shouldn't have any difficulty recognizing this shape, which has a base that is a circle at one end and then tapers to a point at the other end. If your child has never seen a cone before, it's time to break down and take your child out for ice cream.

The ability to recognize each of the shapes described is a fundamental step your child must take to succeed on geometry problems. Along with simple recognition, your child's homework will center around these other activities:

1) Recognition, Explanation, and Comparison

2) Spatial relationships

3) Manipulation of figures

Key Idea: Recognition, Explanation, and Comparison

Your child should be able to look at any of the various figures on pages 60-63 and say, "That's a _____. "

The "explanation" part of the assignment means that your child can use terms such as *length, width, height,* and *edge* correctly. This is one step up from recognition: your child now has to recognize a circle, and then explain what makes it a circle, and not a triangle.

Comparison is one step up from this, since now your child will face a question like

---

EXAMPLE:

How is a square similar to a rectangle? How is it different?

Homework Heroics: Shape of the Day

IF YOUR CHILD has trouble remembering the names of shapes, try this exercise: Every day, pick one shape and review its characteristics. Then play a game where your child earns a point every time he spots that figure. For example, if the shape of the day is a circle, your child could earn one point by spotting a car tire, a quarter, and so forth. For the planar shapes, you could see how fast a player can reach fifty points by seeing fifty different objects. The solid objects might be tougher, so just go for a total number in one day.

If your child is comfortable with the basic figures, this type of homework assignment should be easy. For example, a square and rectangle both have four sides and four corners that meet in right angles. They are different because all sides of a square are equal in length; in a rectangle, opposite sides are of equal length.

Key Idea: Spatial Relationships

These homework questions center around your child's ability to compare the size of different figures, and explain how some figures relate to each other.

EXAMPLE:

Can the circle below fit inside the square, or the square inside the circle?

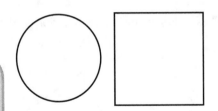

Your child might have some problems with these questions at first. Spatial relationships are something everyone learns with practice, although some people have a better eye for it. To help your child gain this skill, start with easier problems and then make them gradually more difficult. For example, start with a huge circle and a small square. Ask if the square will fit in the circle. Then draw a smaller circle, and ask again, and so on.

To answer this question correctly, your child needs to be able to judge accurately the area of the figures to determine which one will fit in the other one. If she has trouble with that task, get a quarter: the circle is the approximate size of a quarter, so you can place the quarter over the figure of the square to see if it fits.

EXAMPLE:

How many squares (like the one below) will fit into the rectangle without overlapping?

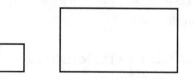

The key here is once again to mentally cut out the square, and then place it into the rectangle as many times as it will fit. Drawing similar-sized squares inside the rectangle is a good way to answer this problem. You should be able to fit two rows of three squares each, so the answer is six.

EXAMPLE:

Yes or No: Is the shaded portion of the triangle greater than or less than the non-shaded portion?

Your child's understanding of the fraction ½ will help her answer this question. Is the shaded area more than half of the triangle, or less? Tell your child to trust her eyes, and give it her best answer. In some ways, this is a comparison question, as your child must compare the shaded portion with the unshaded portion. The shaded portion is less than half of the triangle.

Key Idea: Manipulation of Figures

Now it's time to start spinning, flipping, and slicing all the basic shapes your child has learned. As you might guess, manipulating figures is something that your child will do in the second grade, not kindergarten. He might see an assignment like

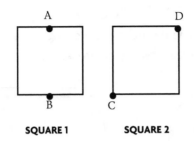

SQUARE 1   SQUARE 2

EXAMPLE A:

Look at Square 1. Now draw a line connecting points A and B.
What new shapes have been created?

EXAMPLE B:

Now draw a line connecting points C and D on Square 2. What
shapes have you created this time?

These straightforward questions illustrate two important concepts of basic geometry: the idea that geometric shapes are made up of
other geometric shapes, and the idea of symmetry. **Symmetry** means
an exact matching of parts on opposite sides of a dividing line or
around a central point.

For Square 1, you can make two rectangles by cutting a square. At
the same time, Square 2 shows that two triangles can be created from
the same kind of square. To paraphrase Freud, "Sometimes a square is
just a square, but that doesn't mean you can't change it into a different geometric figure as well." Okay okay, poor Freud is turning over in
his grave at this point, but the fact remains that understanding the
interaction between different geometric shapes is an important concept.

After both squares are cut by lines AB and CD, the sides opposite
each line are equal in size and shape—they are symmetrical. The two
rectangles are also symmetrical (as are the two triangles).

EXAMPLE B:

Draw a straight line through the following figures in order two create two symmetrical halves.

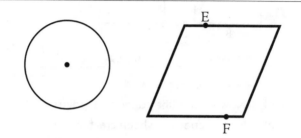

If your child is skeptical of geometric manipulation, spend some time combining different shapes to show various outcomes. For example, two triangles can be combined to make a diamond, six squares can be combined to make a cube, two semicircles can be made into a circle, and so forth. As your child becomes more comfortable with the basic shapes, he will find that manipulating them becomes much easier.

For the circle, since every point along its edge is the same distance from the center, your child just needs to draw a straight line that goes through the center of the circle. The next figure, the diamond, is a little tougher. Your child might want to draw a straight line down the middle, from E to F. However, this doesn't actually create two symmetrical sides. A good way to explain this to your child is to use the Fold Test.

•••••

The Fold Test for Symmetry: After you draw a line through a figure, imagine folding the figure along that line. If the figure is cut symmetrically, then both sides will line up with each other exactly.

•••••

With the diamond, if your child places the line of symmetry between E and F, when he "folds" up the two different sides, he will see that they do not match each other completely. In fact, the two sides of a diamond cut at line EF will have the same size, but they do not have the same shape. You need both in order to have symmetry.

68

Measurement

If you ask your child to come to the supper table and eat, and he responds, "I'll be there in three," that doesn't really mean anything, does it? To be more precise, it could mean a lot of different things: three *seconds* would be very prompt, but three *hours* wouldn't (dinner would definitely be cold by then).

To help avoid such dining disasters, your child will spend his early school years learning the names of all the various units of time, weight/mass, temperature, volume/capacity, and so forth. This section will review all of these elements, discussing both metric and standard units for all of them.

Homework assignments on measurement generally fall into the category of "simple understanding." Your child needs to understand the value of an inch, the duration of an hour, and whether 85 degrees Fahrenheit is warm or cold, for example. This way, if your child's teacher asks, "Can you hold your thumb and forefinger one inch apart?" your child will be able to do this task. If the teacher says, "Recess will begin at 1:00 P.M.," your child will understand that he only has to wait another half-hour to play dodge ball.

However, the first questions your child might ask are, "Why are there two different systems of measurement? Why can't I just learn one?" The explanation provides a good framework for all the different units, so it should be explained.

Key Idea: Metric Versus Standard Units

The best way to explain the difference between these two systems is to tell a story:

Imagine you woke up one morning and a person said that you have to run three miles to the local stadium within thirty minutes. (If you need motivation for this kind of fable, add a million-dollar prize.) You jump out of bed and dress quickly. Unfortunately, all your clothes are in the wash and none of your shoes have laces, so you head out onto the street wearing a bathrobe, dress slacks, a pith helmet, and a pair of fuzzy bunny slippers.

You're making good time, but halfway to the stadium you come across a pair of fine running shoes, as well as a nifty jogging outfit. You now face a dilemma: Do you spend extra time putting on the new-found running shoes and jogging outfit, or do you just continue on in what you were wearing? On one hand, the jogging suit and running shoes make sense, but is the delay worth it?

Most countries in the world took the jogging shoes and outfit, which represent the metric system. The United States stuck with the bunny slippers we were already wearing, which represents the standard system.

The metric system is simpler to use because every unit is divisible by factors of 10, regardless of what system of measurement is being used. For example, the basic unit of length is the *meter,* while the basic unit of capacity is the *liter.* The prefix *deci-* means "tenth," and so 10 *decimeters* = 1 *meter.* What do 10 *deciliters* equal? One liter, of course.

The United States actually adopted a Metric Act in 1975, but conversion isn't exactly moving at a fast pace. If you think converting to the metric system should be easy, just imagine how many speed limit signs there are in America.

The metric system is simple to use. Unfortunately, it hasn't been around for a long time, so prior to its development people came up with all sorts of units—the foot for distance, the pound for weight—and created a great many rules as well (twelve inches equals one foot, three feet equals one yard, and so on). The problem is, you have to know all of the rules in order to measure anything properly.

So while the metric system is simpler to understand and easier to use, old habits—and units of measurement—die hard.

Key Idea: Length

Length is used to measure distance. In the standard system, the basic units of length are

Unit	Meaning
Inch	The smallest unit of length; 1 inch = 1/12 of a foot
Foot	12 inches = 1 foot
Yard	3 feet = 1 yard; 36 inches = 1 yard
Mile	5,280 feet = 1 mile; 1,760 yards = 1 mile

In the metric system, the basic unit of length is the **meter**, which is roughly the same distance as one yard. Here is a breakdown of other lengths. Note that the prefixes are the same throughout the metric system.

Prefix	Meaning	Example
milli–	1/1000	1000 millimeters = 1 meter
centi–	1/100	100 centimeters = 1 meter,
		10 millimeters = 1 centimeter
deci–	1/10	10 decimeters = 1 meter
deka–	10	10 meters = 1 dekameter
hecto–	100	100 meters = 1 hectometer
kilo–	1000	1000 meters = 1 kilometer

On metric conversion problems, everything moves up or down by a factor of 10, so changing units involves either multiplying (or dividing) by 10.

Key Idea: Units of Time

Time is used to measure duration, or how long something lasts. Here are the basic units of time:

The smallest unit of time is the **second**. It should take you about three seconds to read the previous sentence.

Unit	Meaning
1 minute	60 seconds
1 hour	60 minutes
1 day	24 hours
1 year	365 days

*A*ctually, the total number of days in a year is about 365.24, which is why we have a leap year roughly every four years. We have to make up for that pesky little quarter of a day. This won't come up in your child's homework, but it's useful to know if your child asks what a leap year is.

A year is also divided into twelve **months**, which are periods of approximately thirty days. The months of the year are: January, February, March, April, May, June, July, August, September, October, November, and December.

A month can also be split into smaller units, called **weeks**, which are periods of seven days. The days of the week are: Sunday, Monday, Tuesday, Wednesday, Thursday, Friday, and Saturday.

There are roughly four weeks in a month, and fifty-two weeks in every year.

Anything between a *second* and a *year* is fair game by the second grade. By the second grade, your child will also learn to tell time from an analog clock. With this in mind,

•••••

Make sure there is at least one analog clock or watch in your home.

•••••

Digital clocks make nifty bedside alarm/radios, but they won't help your child answer questions about the Big Hand and the Little Hand.

EXAMPLE:

What time is shown on the clock below?

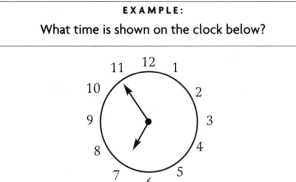

As you might expect, the mistake everyone makes at least once in their lives is to confuse the **hour hand** and the **minute hand**. Since you need the hour (little) hand first, tell your child to think in terms of good manners: start with the little hand, since it's smaller and needs more attention. Then look at the big hand, which doesn't mind waiting around while you check out its smaller relative. The big hand gives the minutes, and there's your answer, 6:55.

> **K**nowing how to tell time on an analog clock also helps children with homework planning (see pages 9-10).

If your child answers 7:55, this is because the hour hand is closer to the seven than the six. This is due to the "sweeping" nature of the clock hands. The hour hand doesn't hit the number 6, and then stay exactly there until 6:59, leaping to 7 one minute later. Instead, it moves slowly in a clockwise manner. Your child should always look at the number that has been passed by a clock hand, and not the number the hand is approaching.

Once your child is comfortable with telling time, the next type of question is the time-elapsation problem. Take the previous problem. If it's 6:55, what time will it be in 15 minutes?

Since your second-grade child has learned his numbers from 1 to 100, numbers larger than 60 aren't unusual to him. This is why your child might give the answer "6:70" for the problem above. Since there

*I*f your child remembers his regrouping exercises from page 52, you can explain this problem using those terms. In effect, 70 minutes = 1 hour 10 minutes, and his job is to "carry" the "1" hour over to the hour number and add it there.

are only 60 minutes in every hour, 70 minutes is not correct. The answer is 7:10.

Key Idea: Units of Weight (or Mass)

Weight (or mass) measures how heavy something is. The standard unit of weight is the **pound**. When you have a lot of pounds, 2,000 to be exact, you have a **ton**. (One pound also equals 16 ounces). To give your child an idea of how much a pound weighs, head to the kitchen. If you have any packaged fruit or meat from a store, the weight is often on the package.

The main unit of mass in the metric system is the **gram**. Based on a gram, your child can then add the metric prefixes on page 71 to go up or down in mass. The **kilogram**, which equals 2.2 pounds, is a standard by which most everyday objects are measured.

Key Idea: Volume (or Capacity)

Volume is the measure of space inside a three-dimensional shape (this is just a fancy way of saying that volume is used to measure liquids).

The standard unit for volume is the **gallon**. Milk is often sold in one-gallon containers.

Unit	Meaning
Pint	2 pints = 1 quart
Quart	4 quarts = 1 gallon
Cup	16 cups = 1 gallon; 4 cups = 1 quart
Ounce	128 ounces = 1 gallon; 8 ounces = 1 cup

In the metric system, the base unit for capacity is the **liter**. Prefixes can then be applied as needed (see chart on page 71).

After slogging though the conversion of cups to quarts to gallons, your child might start to wish that the Metric Act of 1975 was enforced.

Key Idea: Temperature

Temperature measures how hot or cold a substance is. The standard system uses the Fahrenheit scale, while the metric system uses the Celsius scale. In Fahrenheit, water boils at 212 degrees and freezes at 32 degrees (snow day!). In the Celsius scale, 0 degrees is the temperature at which water freezes and 100 degrees is the temperature at which water boils.

Algebra and Patterns

The use of variables in equations like $4x + 6y = 27$ is what many people associate with the word *algebra,* but at the K-2 level the variable concept is too abstract. Instead, the focus is on the idea of replacing the missing piece of an equation, so that algebra homework at this level will resemble something like

---
EXAMPLE:

Write the missing number in the square that makes the equation correct.

$$3 + \square = 5$$

If your child is familiar with basic arithmetic, she should be able to get the correct answer on this problem simply by looking at it. However, there is a method that can be taught if the missing number, 2, is not readily recognized as the answer. The key to this method, called *isolating the unknown,* centers around our old friend, the equal sign (see page 45 for more about it). Whenever you have an equal sign, it means that both sides of the equation (the left side and the right side) have the same value. Therefore, you can add the same number to or subtract the same number from *both* sides of an equation, and you will still have a true equation. In its simplest form, this means

7 = 7 (certainly true)

7 − 2 = 7 − 2 (the same number, 2, is being subtracted from both sides)

5 = 5 (also true)

Of course, you could add 3 to both sides of 5 = 5, and you would get 8 = 8, which is also true.

Once your child gets comfortable with this idea, go back to the problem. To find the missing piece of the equation, you need to get rid of everything that's on the same side of the equation as the unknown (the number that goes in the square). Therefore, you must subtract 3 from both sides of the equation. Now the square is all by itself on one side of the equation, so all you have to do is subtract 3 from 5 on the other side of the equation to get your answer, 2.

$$3 + \square = 5$$
$$3 - 3 + \square = 5 - 3 \text{ (subtracting 3 from both sides)}$$
$$\square = 2$$

If your child is unconvinced, go back to the original problem, insert a 2 into the square, and determine whether 3 + 2 = 5 is the correct answer.

As you might imagine, manipulating an equation—adding and subtracting to find the value of a missing number—is a skill that your child will use again and again. But even in the second grade, the equations are rarely more advanced than the previous question, so don't push your child to understand greater abstractions.

Key Idea: Word Problems

In the previous example, the equation was presented to your child, and his job was to solve for the missing number. A similar type of problem is the word problem, which requires your child to set up the equation and then solve it.

EXAMPLE:

Kylie is counting the number of hats she owns. She discovers that she has 13 baseball caps, 3 cowboy hats, and 1 winter hat. How many hats does Kylie have in all?

To get this problem right, you have to decide what numbers need to be added or subtracted. Here's some advice:

•••••

When faced with a word problem, set up the equation using words; next, add the numbers into the equation, and then do the math last.

•••••

In this example, you have to find the total number of hats. First, you should list all the different types of hats mentioned in the problem: baseball, cowboy and winter.

baseball   cowboy   winter = total

To find the total, you have to decide whether to add or subtract the hats. To find a total, addition is required.

baseball hats + cowboy hats + winter hats = total
13 + 3 + 1 =
16 + 1 =
17 = total number of hats Kylie owns

The advantage of the first step, using only the words, is that it will give your child a better chance to determine the proper arithmetic procedure needed. Your child can think about physical objects (hats) instead of abstract values (numbers). This makes it easier to set up the problem correctly. Once that step is complete, your child can then shift from the concrete objects to the abstract values.

Here is a tougher algebra word problem. It even includes a minor time-elapse element, making it something only a second-grader would see.

EXAMPLE:

At 2:00 P.M. Michael had 15 cherry tomatoes. He ate four cherry tomatoes every hour. At 3:00 P.M., how many cherry tomatoes remained?

This problem has two steps, but you can still set up the equation without using numbers.

number of tomatoes to begin with +/− tomatoes eaten = tomatoes remaining

Then you need to decide whether to add or subtract the number of tomatoes eaten in order to find out the number of tomatoes remaining. *Remaining* is the key word here, so subtraction must be used. The step that makes this problem a tough one is the fact that you must figure that the number of tomatoes eaten is 4, since Michael eats 4 an hour and one hour has passed. After that, the translation of words to numbers occurs, and the problem becomes $15 - 4 = 11$ tomatoes remaining.

Another advantage to working word problems this way is that questions like these often ask for the answer in a variety of forms. For example, this question asks, "How many cherry tomatoes remained?" However, the question could just as easily be, "Set up the proper equation to show how many cherry tomatoes remain," or "Draw a picture to show how many tomatoes remain." Both of these questions ask for the same math information, but they require different answer types. The first question could be answered, "Michael had 15 tomatoes, but he ate 4 of them between 2 P.M. and 3 P.M. He should have only 11 tomatoes remaining." This is the same answer, but your child had to explain his answer in words. A pictorial solution would be for your child to draw 15 tomatoes (circles), cross out four of them, leaving 11 tomatoes remaining.

Having your child set up the equation using words should allow him to gain a better understanding of what the problem is asking. This comes in handy when the question asks for something more than just a numerical answer.

Key Idea: Patterns

There are two main types of pattern problems: mathematic and visual. The mathematic patterns are typically addition and subtraction patterns, not unlike the counting concept discussed on pages 46-47. Homework assignments for patterns usually consist of a list of numbers where your child has to figure out the next number in the sequence, or what a missing number might be.

EXAMPLE:

Look at the following series of numbers:

22, 19, 16, 13, 10, _____

What number comes next?

Pattern problems are often grouped with algebra because the key to understanding the pattern is figuring out the missing mathematical operation. In algebra it's a missing number, but with a pattern it's a missing operation.

*****

With a number pattern, take any two numbers next to each other and determine what has been added or subtracted to get from the left number to the right number.

*****

In the example, take the first two numbers, 22 and 19. To get from the left number (22) to the right number (19), you have to subtract 3. That's the pattern! The number in the blank space would then be 10 − 3 = 7, so 7 is the answer.

To make sure a pattern is correct, your child can always test two sets of numbers. Testing 22 and 19 gives him "subtract 3" as the pattern, but to check this, he can take any other pair, such as 16 and 13. Is the pattern the same? If it is, that's confirmation that "subtract 3" is the pattern being followed.

Addition and subtraction will be the main patterns in kindergarten through second grade, but multiplication and division will follow in later grades.

Visual patterns are just what you might expect: a series of repeating icons, or symbols, that follow a certain pattern. The following method won't always work, but it is a very effective first approach.

*****

For a visual pattern, take a good look at the first icon. Then look at each object to the right of it until you find that first icon again. Once you do, everything between the first icon and its second appearance is usually the visual pattern.

*****

EXAMPLE:

Look at the following pattern and decide what symbol comes next.

★ ❄ ✎ ✋ ★ ❄ ✎ ✋ ★ ❄ ✎ _____

Take the first icon, and let's call it "star." Proceeding to the right, your child will encounter "snowflake," "pencil," "hand," and then "star" again. Stop! There's the pattern: star, snowflake, pencil, then hand. The pattern then repeats—that's what patterns do, after all—and you have star, snowflake, pencil . . . so the answer is *hand*. Victory!

For the most part, young students have trouble with visual patterns because they just look so strange. However, if your child learns how to approach them methodically, she should have no trouble finding the pattern every time.

Computation and Analysis

nother title for this section could be "Charts and Graphs." Charts and graphs are alternate ways to display numerical information or data. They are used quite often in mathematics and pop up in all sorts of other places as well—newspaper articles, presentations, baseball games, and even game shows. (Contrary to any rumors you might have heard, they do not grow wild in nature.)

Key Idea: Charts

Charts are the simplest form of visual information. A simple chart is a grid pattern made up of horizontal rows and vertical columns. For example, suppose you had three children, Albert, Bertram, and Claude, who picked apples from Monday through Friday. A chart showing their apple-picking abilities could look like the one below.

Apples Picked

	Mon	Tues	Wed	Thurs	Fri
Albert	13	21	6	9	14
Bertram	32	27	16	14	21
Claude	11	9	5	18	10

In this chart, the vertical columns represent the days of the week, while the horizontal rows show the numbers of apples picked by each child.

Understanding what the rows and columns represent is the first step when reading any chart.

Homework questions about this chart might be as simple as

EXAMPLE:
How many apples did Bertram pick on Wednesday?

With some practice your child will be able to read a chart with her eyes alone. However, if she seems hesitant about her abilities, start her off with the Two-Finger Method. On the Bertram/Wednesday question, have her place her left forefinger on the name Bertram, and her right forefinger on the column, Wednesday. Now, she should move her left forefinger straight across the page, and her right forefinger straight down the page, until the two forefingers meet. They can only move in straight lines! The two fingers will meet at 16, which is the number of apples Bertram picked on Wednesday. The Two-Finger method is always effective, but once your child gets comfortable with charts she probably will not need it.

To find the answer, your child would go to the row titled *Bertram,* and read across until he reaches the *Wednesday* column. The number in this rectangle is the number of apples Bertram picked on Wednesday, 16.

By the second grade, however, merely reading a chart will not be all that is required. Instead, simple analysis of the information will now be an additional part of an assignment. Simple analysis means that your child is able to take the numbers in the chart, and then perform simple calculations with them, such as

---

EXAMPLE A:
How many apples did Albert pick for the entire week?

---

or

EXAMPLE B:
How many apples were picked on Thursday?

Both questions employ a bit of chart reading, and then some algebra skills as your child must create the correct equation to get the right answer. On the first question, for instance, the proper equation would be:

$$13 + 21 + 6 + 9 + 14 = \text{total number of apples picked by Albert}$$
$$= 63$$

If your child doesn't understand where those five numbers came from, go back to the first step, which would be to write out "number of apples Albert picked Monday" + "number of apples Albert picked Tuesday," and so on, which would equal the number of apples he picked that week.

The second question also requires addition, but this time your child would have to add down the column *Thursday,* $9 + 14 + 8 = 31$, to get the right answer.

Key Idea: Graphs

While charts are predominately all numbers and headings, graphs contain a pictorial element to them.

Number of Snails Sighted

	1	2	3	4	5	6
Kendall	🐌	🐌	🐌			
Abraham	🐌	🐌				
Kronhorst	🐌	🐌	🐌	🐌	🐌	

In this graph, the names of the various children are written down the side, and the number of snails they spotted is listed along the top edge. As you see, this easier **pictorial graph** allows your child to count the objects (and not just use the numbers along the type) to answer a question like

Some children might wonder why anyone would use a bar graph when a pictorial graph is so much easier to read. The fact is that a bar graph has certain advantages, in the sense that anyone even casually glancing at the bar graph will know that Kronhorst saw the most butterflies, since the bar coming out from Kronhorst's name is larger than the other two.

EXAMPLE:

How many snails did Kronhorst see?

There are two ways to answer this problem. First, your child can just count the snails listed. Or, she can scan her eyes out to the right until she reaches Kronhorst's last snail, and then she can scan upward to read the number 5 above it. This shows that Kronhorst saw five snails.

While the first method works fine for pictorial graphs, as you might guess, many graphs are not pictorial. Instead, they are called **bar graphs**, and they can be read only by the second method. Here is bar graph of the same snail information.

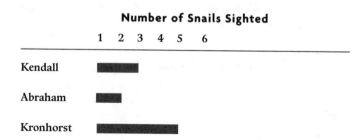

Number of Snails Sighted

The same information is shown, only now the abstract gray-striped bar has taken the place of the snail placeholders. To find out how many snails Kronhorst saw, your child would scan with his eyes over to the far right edge of Kronhorst's bar, and then scan upward to read the number 5 above it. Ta da!

Key Idea: Making Bar Graphs (Second Grade Only)

Your second-grader might be asked to construct a simple bar graph. Don't panic: the graph won't be very long or involved.

The key to graph-making is proper labeling. Look back on the apple-picking chart on page 81. Suppose your child's assignment is:

EXAMPLE:

Create a bar graph that shows how many apples each child picked on Wednesday.

First, your child needs to decide what he wants to list down the graph, and what he wants to list across the top. Since the name of the kids are in rows, why not keep it that way? Then, taking a page from the snail bar graph on page 84, list the numbers along the top. Your child's bar graph should be set up like this:

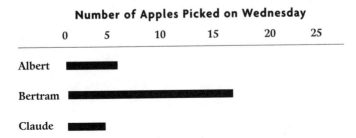

Number of Apples Picked on Wednesday

	0	5	10	15	20	25

Albert

Bertram

Claude

The numbers along the top are in multiples of 5, but your child can come up with a different system if he prefers. The main point here is that the most apples picked on Wednesday was 16, so the graph has to extend at least to 16. If it didn't, Bertram's bar would spill over.

As it is, with the correct set-up, all that is left to do is fill in the bars. Albert picked 6 apples on Wednesday, so your child can either start drawing a bar out of the 0 along Albert's line, and then stop when the bar is directly where the 6 would be on the top; or, he can start with the numbers, heading out to where the 6 is. He would then drop down from there to Albert's row, make a line, and then fill in everything from that line towards Albert's name until 0 is reached.

Either system will help your child create a bar graph.

CHAPTER 3

A Review of Basic K-2
English Concepts

ENGLISH—ALSO CALLED ENGLISH LANGUAGE ARTS in some parts of the country—can be broken down into four main categories: Phonics, Grammar, Writing, and Reading. What follows is a review of the major concepts and ideas that are the foundation of basic English instruction. You will be familiar with most of these topics, but you might have forgotten some of the terminology involved.

Phonics

Phonics is the study of speech sounds. At the kindergarten through second-grade level, phonics is the way children learn to associate letters and words with their sound values (or spoken

Homework Heroics: Teaching Kids to Love Reading

THE SINGLE MOST important thing you can do to improve your child's English skills is to encourage your child to read as much as possible. Reading pretty much any kind of book or magazine is better than not reading at all. If your child enjoys Dr. Seuss, let her read Dr. Seuss. If she likes reading about gophers, by all means get her copies of <u>Burrow Monthly</u>. The more exposure children have to books, the more comfortable they become with reading, writing, and grammar.

Reading provides children with good language models. They see and hear in their inner ear (the inner ear you "hear" words with when you read) correctly written sentences put together in moving and interesting ways. This helps your child actually internalize the rules of grammar. She will develop the ability to look at a sentence and determine almost instinctively whether it's written correctly, because she knows what proper prose looks like.

A further discussion about reading skills is covered on page 111-117.

values). Think about the word *cat:* as adults, we know how to say *cat,* but your child will learn by practicing the hard *c* sound, the soft *a* sound, and then the *t* sound. Putting those three sounds together, you get *cat,* and you have just used phonics.

Key Idea: The Alphabet

Before your child learns how to pronounce all the different letters of the alphabet, he first has to learn what those letters are. The twenty-six letters of the alphabet can all be found in the sentence

The quick brown fox jumps over the lazy dog.

The best way to help your child memorize the alphabet is to sing that song, you know, the one that goes "A B C D E F G . . . " Well, you probably know the lyrics, since the lyrics are the alphabet. If your child is having trouble with alphabet assignments, you can give him extra practice by making (or buying) flashcards. Put one letter of the alphabet on each card, and then several pictures of items that begin with that letter. For example, a flashcard for the letter *d* might have a picture of a dog, a dish, and a drum; these images will help your child make associations with the letter.

The alphabet is broken up into two groups: vowels and consonants. A **vowel** is a speech sound made with almost no blocking of the flow of air through the throat and mouth; a **consonant** is a speech sound made by partly or completely blocking the flow of air through the throat and mouth. Your child won't need to define these terms, but he will need to recognize a letter and know whether it is a vowel or a consonant. More importantly, he will need to look at the letter and know how to pronounce it—after all, that's the point of phonics in the first place.

The letter y is sometimes a consonant, but it is also occasionally used as a vowel, as in fly or cycle. It can have either a long i or a short i sound.

The vowels

There are five vowels: *a, e, i, o,* and *u*. Each vowel has what is known as a "short sound" and a "long sound." Here is a chart with some examples of each.

Vowel	Long sound	Short sound
A	bake	cat
E	these	cell
I	smile	big
O	note	box
U	mule	fun

When learning phonics, it is crucial that your child have access to a dictionary. The pronunciation key for every word is the first thing

One way to help your child remember the long vowels is to say, "The long vowel says its name." When your child recites the alphabet out loud, all of the vowels are pronounced with the long vowel sound.

listed. The long vowel sound is denoted by a bar over the vowel, like $\bar{a}$. The short vowel is denoted by a curved line above the vowel, like $\breve{a}$. Therefore, if your child is unsure of whether to use the long sound or the short sound, you can help him refer to the dictionary for the answer.

The consonants

The remaining twenty-one letters are the consonants. Like vowels, consonants can be pronounced differently in different words. Looking at the preceding chart, you can see that *cat* and *cell* both have *c* in them, but there is a **hard** *c* in *cat* and a **soft** *c* in *cell*. Other consonants, such as *g,* also have hard and soft sounds (*gate* and *giraffe,* respectively).

Homework assignments about phonics are somewhat problematic, since the oral component of language makes it hard for teachers to gauge progress ("Here is the tape of my pronunciations, Mrs. Baba"). Still, one type of assignment might involve checking to see if your child understands the long and short vowel symbols.

EXAMPLE:
Does the word *wheel* use a long *e* or a short *e* sound?

By saying the word *wheel* out loud, your child should recognize the long *e* sound.

EXAMPLE:
See it: flūt. Speak it:_____.

In this example, your child is given the pronunciation of a word and then asked to speak it. This is the kind of drill that will also go on in the classroom. Learning how to say words correctly based on their phonetic spelling is integral to understanding phonics. The question here is fairly straightforward; with the long *u* sound, your child should say the word *flute.*

Key Idea: Digraphs, Diphthongs, and Syllables

The first two words, *digraphs* and *diphthongs,* sound a lot tougher than their meaning. Basically, both mean "a combination of letters that form a single sound." A **digraph**, though, is a combination of two letters that are used to represent one sound. Some digraphs are: the *ch-* sound in *chin* and the *-ng* sound in *wing.* **Diphthongs** are usually two vowels, or one vowel along with a *w* or a *y,* that combine to form a special combined sound. Examples include the *-oy* in boy and the *-ou* sound in *house.*

Frankly, the English language is lousy with digraphs and diphthongs (the underlined letters are just some of them). The best way to learn all of them is simply through continued exposure to the English language (i.e., *reading!*). Reading out loud (with a dictionary nearby) is a great way to boost your child's English skills and phonetic ability.

If faced with a word like *clownish,* your child will discover the diphthong *-ow* that creates the combined sound *-au.* The phonetic spelling would be something like

klau • nish

A neat way to figure out how many syllables are in a word is by placing your hand underneath your jaw and then saying the word. Every time you feel your jaw drop down towards your hand, that shows a break between syllables. In fact, if you say a word very slowly, you can often figure out where the exact syllable break occurs by feeling when your hand starts to rise back up.

Notice the dot between the *u* and the *n*? That shows the break between **syllables** in the word *clownish.* A syllable is just a unit of a spoken word that consists of one or more letters. The syllables tell you how the units of letters are spoken; for example, if you changed things so that the syllable break was at *klaun • ish,* then you would say the word differently. The change is subtle, but important nonetheless.

Key Idea: Synonyms, Antonyms, Homonyms, and Homophones

Your child may encounter drills and exercises involving the following four terms:

Term	Definition	Example
Synonym	Two words with similar meaning	*big* and *large*
Antonym	Two words with opposite meaning	*hot* and *cold*
Homonym	Two words that are spelled the same way and sound alike but have different meanings	*park* (a car) and *park* (an outdoor place)
Homophones	Two words that sound the same but are spelled differently and have different meanings	*blue* and *blew*

Of these four terms, homophones are the most useful when teaching your child phonics, because they show how different groups of letters often make the same sound. Words like *threw* and *through* sound the same, and they show your child that both the *-ew* and *-ough* can be used to create the long *u* sound. Armed with this knowledge, if your child is asked to spell the word *crew,* she knows that two possible spellings are *crew* and *crough,* since both those combinations create the proper phonetic sound. Which of the spellings is correct is often determined by the origin of the word itself (German, Latin, Greek, Sanskrit), which is why there are so many different combinations in the first place.

The other three terms—antonyms, synonyms, and homonyms—are useful tools for building your child's vocabulary. Learning a ton of synonyms for the word *great* allows her to express herself more clearly and become a better writer. It also helps her understand the various relationship between words, providing another way of grouping and categorizing words in her head.

EXAMPLE:

The day was *cold* and *wet.*

First, rewrite the sentence using synonyms for the italicized words. Then write the sentence using antonyms for the italicized words.

Although the word *thesaurus* sounds like the name of a dinosaur, it is in fact a reference book that lists synonyms and antonyms for many words. As you might imagine, having a thesaurus makes homework assignments involving these concepts much easier to complete. At the kindergarten through second-grade level, your child does not need to have her own thesaurus, but it is a good idea to show her one, either at home or at the library. Just knowing that there is a book that contains a listing of synonyms and antonyms is important knowledge for your child, since this reference skill will come up in the future.

For the first part of the problem, your child will have to come up with synonyms for *cold* and *wet,* something like, "The day was *chilly* and *damp.*" Learning that *cold* and *chilly* mean essentially the same thing gives your child the ability to use either word when speaking. For the second part, your child must come up with antonyms to describe the opposite of *cold* and *wet.* That day should be *"hot* and *dry."*

Homonyms show the limitations of phonics: even though you hear the word correctly and can spell it properly, that does not mean you know what its exact meaning is. The word *set* has about sixty different meanings, and in order to figure out which meaning is being used, your child has to look at the entire sentence. Any discussion of complete sentences invariably brings us to the topic of grammar.

Grammar

*I*f a large pharmaceutical company developed a pill that, once swallowed, would give everyone perfect grammar skills, there would be a long line of people waiting at the door with tall glasses of water in their hands (and the authors of this book would be among them).

A great deal of English grammar contradicts itself; on some levels it's fairly coherent, but on other levels it's illogical. Here is some advice for your child.

• • • • •

Understand the basics of grammar—subject/verb agreement, proper capitalization and spelling, for example—and look up anything you do not know in a grammar reference book.

• • • • •

Make sure your child has a reputable, age-appropriate grammar book on hand—the more comprehensive the better. Once you find a book you and your child like, encourage him to:

1) Use it continuously and aggressively

2) Learn from his mistakes

If you can convince your child to look up grammar rules whenever he is unsure of the correct rule, you will have made an important step. The next step is to get your child to understand his own errors. Here is one way to make sure this happens:

• • • • •

Maintain a list called "Common Grammar Mistakes," and have your child jot down one or two, along with the correct grammar rules, whenever he receives an assignment back from the teacher with mistakes highlighted. Have him use it as a reference sheet and keep it in his homework location.

• • • • •

English grammar rules evolved over time. The same should happen with your child, with his knowledge of correct grammar being built on a steady succession of mistakes corrected.

Homework Heroics: Be a Good Model

IT MAY BE a pain to mind your grammar when you are just relaxing at home, but if you can provide your child with a good spoken language model at all times, you will be doing him a great service. First of all, by speaking grammatically, you help your child internalize the rules of grammar. Secondly, by speaking correctly, you encourage your child to speak correctly, too, which will set him on the road to success in kindergarten and beyond. Remember your own mother correcting you whenever you said "ain't"? Well, she had the right idea.

Key Idea: Forming Complete Sentences

A **sentence** describes a complete idea. Every sentence is composed of two parts: the subject and the predicate.

The subject of a sentence contains either a noun or a pronoun, while the predicate contains a verb. For more discussion about nouns, pronouns, and verbs, turn to pages 106-108.

The **subject** tells who or what the sentence is about.

The **predicate** tells what the subject is or what it does.

Therefore, "the gray dog" is not a sentence. The gray dog could be the subject of a sentence, but there's no predicate. If you add "runs through the forest," then you have, "The gray dog runs through the forest." This is a complete sentence, because it has a subject, *the gray dog,* that tells what the sentence is about, and a predicate, *runs through the forest,* that tells what the subject did.

Incomplete sentences are known as **sentence fragments**. Your child's homework assignments will focus on forming proper sentences and recognizing and fixing sentence fragments.

EXAMPLE:

Which of the following are sentence fragments?

A. Johnny went to the store.

B. Knows few people at school.

C. The science teacher Mr. Klondike.

In order to have a complete sentence, you need to find a subject and a predicate. If either one is missing, it's a fragment. On part A, there is a subject, *Johnny*, that tells who the sentence is about; the predicate, *went to the store*, shows what Johnny did. Complete sentence!

B and C are fragments, since B is missing a subject and C is missing a predicate. If you combine C with B (in that order), you now have a complete sentence.

For more about the various parts of speech that make up a sentence, turn to pages 106-111.

In the second grade, the list of capitalization rules will expand as your child learns about capitalizing titles, certain parts of a letter, and words that start a direct quote.

Key Idea: Capitalization

To paraphrase Hamlet, this topic boils down to the question, "To *B* or not to *b*?" In other words, when is the uppercase letter used to start a word, and when is the lowercase letter used? At the kindergarten through second-grade level, your child will be taught to capitalize the first letter of a word:

1) At the beginning of every sentence

2) When using the pronoun *I*

3) When using a specific name (a proper noun)

Of these three, the first two are fairly straightforward. Always start a sentence with a capital letter on the first letter of the first word, and never write *i* when referring to oneself (use *I* instead). As for the third

*I*nterestingly enough, the terms uppercase *and* lowercase *have their origin in early typesetting practices. Typesetters would keep wooden blocks of each letter in two holding cases. The capital letters were stored in the upper case, while the lower letters were kept in the lower case. Since then, the practice of calling capitalized letters "uppercase" has stuck.*

In addition to the history lesson, this anecdote might provide a good way for your child to remember the difference between upper and lowercase.

rule, the topic of proper nouns is covered on page 106, but basically it means the first letter of a word referring to a specific person, place, or thing is always capitalized. The First Rule of Sparky provides a good explanation of proper nouns:

The First Rule of Sparky

If you tell someone that dogs like to play, you are talking about dogs in general; you're not referring to any one dog in particular. Therefore, the word *dogs* is not capitalized. However, if you tell someone that your dog, Sparky, likes to play, then you are referring to a specific dog—in this case, Sparky—so the word is a proper noun and must be capitalized.

EXAMPLE:

Capitalize the appropriate letters in the following sentences:
Jonas walked up to me. he asked me where i was going. jonas is my friend. I told jonas i was going to the park.

There are several words that need to be capitalized in this question, one for each of the rules listed at the beginning of this section. The pronoun *I*, in the second and fourth sentence, is always capitalized; remembering Sparky, the name *Jonas* refers to a specific person, so the *J* in Jonas should be capitalized every time it appears; *he*, which starts the second sentence, must also be capitalized because it is the first word in that sentence.

Key Idea: Punctuation

Building proper, basic sentences is a key part of kindergarten through second-grade grammar, so in addition to a subject and a predicate, your child will also learn that every sentence has to end with some form of punctuation. Following is a chart of the four basic sentence types and the appropriate end punctuation for each one.

The Four Basic Sentence Types

1. SENTENCE TYPE   **Declarative**

Definition	Declarative sentences make a statement or explain something.
Example	Our town is very pretty.
End With a	Period (.)

2. SENTENCE TYPE   **Interrogative**

Definition	Interrogative sentences ask questions.
Example	Whose book is that?
End With a	Question mark (?)

3. SENTENCE TYPE   **Imperative**

Definition	Imperative sentences give a command or make a request.
Example	Get me a new pair of bowling shoes from the mall.
End With a	Normally, imperative statements end with a period (.). However, if the statement is urgent—*Get these rattlesnakes off of me!*—an exclamation mark (!) may be used.

4. SENTENCE TYPE   Exclamatory

Definition	Exclamatory sentences show surprise or strong feeling.
Example	I just won the lottery!
End With an	Exclamation mark (!)

Most sentences are either declarative or interrogative, so your child will be expected to understand the difference between the two and then use the appropriate punctuation mark. With imperative statements, deciding whether or not to use an exclamation mark or a period is up to the writer and it depends on the larger context. The imperative sentence, "Bring me some gum," should probably end with a period, but if it occurs within the book, *The Vampire From Space Who Feared Gum*, then the statement might be, "Bring me some gum!"

Once your child has figured out the correct end punctuation, it's time to delve into the sentence itself and deal with punctuation there.

Since *The Vampire From Space Who Feared Gum is the* title of a book, the first letter of each word within the title is capitalized.

Commas and Apostrophes

Commas and apostrophes are two types of punctuation that your child will be introduced to by second grade. However, only the basic idea behind both types of punctuation will be introduced, with more in-depth work coming in later grades.

A **comma** is used to indicate a pause and help make a sentence clear. To illustrate this idea, ask your child to repeat this sentence, "It was very very very very hard for me." As he says it, you can note the slight pause after each *very*. There should be a comma wherever the pause occurs, which is why the sentence is correctly written: "It was very, very, very, very hard for me."

Your child will learn to use a comma at the following times:

1) In a series of three or more items (hamburgers, French fries, and a milkshake)

2) To separate two or more adjectives (the big, red balloon)

3) Between a city and a state written next to each other (Chicago, IL)

There are other rules for using a comma, such as after introductory words in a sentence (Yes, dear) or before the conjunction in a compound sentence, but your child will not need to know these rules yet.

EXAMPLE:

Place commas in the following sentences to make them grammatically correct:

A. My father was born in St. Louis Missouri.

B. Be sure to bring hammers nails and wrenches to the construction site.

St. Louis is a city in the state of *Missouri,* so be sure to place a comma between them. In part B, there is a list of three items: *hammers, nails,* and *wrenches.* Therefore, commas should be placed after *hammers* and *nails,* to set off the items in the list. There's no comma after *wrenches* because the list is over.

Apostrophes are used in contractions and to show possession. Children like shortcuts, so your child should have no trouble understanding the idea behind contractions.

Contractions are a shortcut in English. They are made by joining two words together, using an apostrophe, to make a shorter word. Contractions are most frequently made by joining a word to the word *not* and shortening it to *-n't.* For example, *should not* becomes *shouldn't.*

This seems fairly simple, but there's always something that makes it a little difficult. Certain word groups can't (can not) be contracted, such as changing *am not* to *amn't.* Also, the contraction can sometimes change the first of the two words being joined. Your child might think that *will not* would become *willn't*, but in fact the correct word is *won't*.

That's it for Apostrophe 101. Things get trickier in the second grade, since around that time your child will also learn the basics about using apostrophes to show possession.

Possession refers to who owns a particular object. An apostrophe is used to show ownership when it is combined with an *s*.

> **T**he verb is *can also be* shortened to *'s* and then joined with the word before it. For example, *there is can be shortened* to *there's*.

If only one person has ownership, use *'s*. (Jackie's car).

If more than one person has ownership, use *s'*. (the twins' card collection).

Apostrophes that show possession are more difficult than contractions for two reasons. First, your child must figure out whether to use *'s* or *s'*. Second, *'s* is also used when contracting the word *is*, so your child must look at an *'s* and decide whether it is a contraction or if it is showing possession.

EXAMPLE:

Rewrite the following phrases using apostrophes.

A. the hay of the horses

B. the razor of Occam

In part A, who owns the hay? Does it belong to just one horse, or several? Since the hay is for several horses, it should be *the horses' hay*. Only one person owns the razor, though, so it's *Occam's razor*.

If your child looks at the phrase "it's Occam's razor" and understands that the first apostrophe is a contraction and the second one shows possession by one person, then she knows her stuff.

Key Idea: Spelling

There are thousands of different spelling rules, and most rules have exceptions, as well. Your child will probably have one or two homework assignments that focus on a particular rule. In general, learning how to spell words correctly is more important than learning each and every spelling rule. This is why the focus is usually on Spelling (and Vocabulary) tests, not Spelling Rule tests. And that's why spelling involves a lot of memorization.

Knowing some basic rules can help your child when he's attempting to spell a new word for the first time, and it helps to remember sets of words (such as words ending in a particular suffix, such as *-logy*.) Following are some general spelling rules and some tips for helping your child learn new words.

Short and Long Vowel Sounds

Certain letters and letter combinations regularly produce the same sound, regardless of what word they appear in. Since short and long vowel sounds are a key topic in phonics (see pages 87-91), here are some spelling variations that go along with short and long vowel sounds.

Vowel	Short Sounds	Examples
A	a, ai, au	bag, plaid, laugh
E	e, ea, a, ai, ay, ie, u, ue	bed, bread, any
I	i, y, e, ie, o, ee, u, ui	fit, guild, busy
O	o, a	dog, false
U	u, o, ou, a, oe, oo	rug, some, flood

Vowel	Long Sounds	Examples
A	a, ai, ay	plane, plain, way
E	e, ea, ee, or ey (if the *-ey* is at the end of a word)	me, neat, fleet, key
I	i, ie, y, igh	mind, lie, why, tight
O	o, oa, oe, or ow	zone, boat, toe, row
U	u, ue, oo	muse, true, balloon

Prefixes, Suffixes, and Word Roots

One way to increase your child's ability to spell is to teach her Latin. What? You mean you don't know Latin? Well, about 99.999 percent of the world's population is in the same boat as you. However, a large number of English words have Latin roots, or origins. For example, the Latin word for water is *aqua*, and the English word *aquarium* (which means a container that holds water) derives its meaning from the original Latin word.

This is why learning Latin would help anyone's vocabulary and spelling skills. By understanding the original root word, your child has a better shot of understanding any word with the root *aqua* in it. Therefore, if your child heard the word *aquatic*, she should know how to spell the first four letters, and she should also know that the word has something to do with water.

Many English words do not have a Latin origin, however, so don't worry about learning Latin. The main point is to get your child to recognize and understand certain word parts when she sees them. For example, if she learns the word part *bi-* means two, she stands a good chance of understanding the word *bilevel* when she sees it for the first time. If she knows that *tri-* means three, she will know the meaning of *tricycle*.

In the above paragraph, *bi-* and *tri-* are prefixes. A **prefix** is a group of letters (or just one letter) that has the same meaning whenever it appears. Prefixes always appear at the beginning of a word. The prefix *bi-* means "two," so even if your child does not know the exact meaning of the word *bicuspid*, she will at least know that it means "two of something," or "two cuspids." Also, she should have a good chance of spelling the word correctly since the *bi-* is always spelled the same way.

Suffixes are very similar to prefixes, except suffixes appear at the end of a word. Some well-known suffixes are *-logy*, *-able*, and *-wise*.

Spelling and Syllables

When your child gets ready to spell the word *doghouse,* in effect she is spelling two smaller words and then joining them together. This **com-**

pound word has two distinct syllables, *dog* and *house*. When you see a word like *spoken*, you don't try to say all six letters in one quick rush; instead, you say the first three letters, *spo-*, and then the last three, *-ken*. Pronoucing each syllable, and then thinking about how each syllable could be spelled, can make large words easier to handle. This is easily demonstrated using the well-known Mary Poppins song: ask your child to spell *supercalifragilisticexpialidocious*. The prospect seems daunting, but if you go two syllables at a time, your child can come up with a spelling that is reasonably accurate. It is thirty-four letters long, so the chances of spelling it perfectly are fairly low.

Adding Plural Endings

A simple rule involves adding *-es* or *-s* to a word to change it from singular (one) to plural (many). For most words, your child should add a single *-s*, so that *dog* becomes *dogs* and *steamship* becomes *steamships*. However, if a word ends in the letters *h, o, s* and *x* or the letter combinations *-ch* or *-sh,* then the suffix *-es* is added, so that *fox* becomes *foxes* and *hatch* becomes *hatches*.

This same spelling rule applies regardless of why -s or -es is being added. To change a first person present tense verb to third person singular, you would add -s or -es, so that catch becomes catches. As you might imagine, this is way, way above the kindergarten through second-grade level, but it does show your child that if you are adding -s or -es to a word, only add -es if the word ends in an h, o, s, x, -ch or -sh.

EXAMPLE:

Add *-s* or *-es* to the following words:

Tiger, box, crab, beach, box, bus, domino

For *tiger* and *crab,* a simple *-s* ending is needed. The other four words require *-es* endings. Furthermore, the plural for *bus* is sometimes spelled *busses,* with an extra *s* added.

This just illustrates that while spelling rules are helpful, they are not absolute.

Some words change dramatically when converted to plural form. Mouse, for example, becomes mice. These irregualr plurals must simply be memorized.

Adding plurals that change the spelling of the original word

Sometimes adding letters to form a plural isn't as easy as just tacking on an *-s* or *-es*. In the case of many words ending in *y*, for example, the *y* is changed to an *i* before the plural ending is added. This means that *baby* becomes *babies*, and *tricky* becomes *trickies*. Okay, *trickies* is not a real word, but if it were, it would be a good way to describe the fact that some words have tricky plurals. Many words ending in *-f* also have a change in spelling: the *f* transforms into a *v* and then the plural ending is added. This makes *scarf* become *scarves*.

Adding -er and -est to make comparisons

Adding these two suffixes is a common practice in early schooling, since children often work with making comparisons. When only two items are compared, the suffix *-er* is used to show degree, as in, "The blue car is fast*er* than the red one." When three or more items are being compared, the suffix *-est* is used, so, "The blue car is the fast*est* of the three cars."

One way to help your child remember when to add an extra consonant is to talk to them about the Lonely Letters. Some letters, like g and t in this case, are Lonely Letters that like to have company. That's why an extra g is added at the end of bigger, and an extra t is added to words like fattest.

Again, things are never as simple as adding *-er* and *-est* in every situation. In some cases, the *y* is replaced by an *i*, and therefore *busy* becomes *busier.* In other instances, an extra consonant is added at the end before the *-er* and *-est*, so that *big* becomes *bigger* and and *fat* becomes *fattest.*

Expect your child to make many mistakes when learning proper spelling. The English language is full of bizarre letter combinations. The best way for your child to learn how to spell words properly is to learn from his mistakes.

Key Idea: The Eight Parts Of Speech

All words in the English language can be placed into one of these eight categories, so knowing about them is critical. The key parts of speech at this level are: noun, pronoun, verb, adjective, and adverb. The remaining three parts of speech—interjections, conjunctions, and prepositions—are not as integral at this stage, but they will be touched on briefly just in case your child does run into them.

Noun—A noun names a person, place, thing, or idea in a sentence. *Dog, forest,* and *joy* are all nouns.

There are two main categories of nouns: common nouns and proper nouns. A **common noun** represents one or all members of a group of persons, places, or things. *Neighbor, house,* and *beach* are all common nouns. A **proper noun** names a specific member of a common group of persons, places or things, so *Mrs. Parkinson, Lake Erie,* and *Bubbly Cola* are all proper nouns. See the First Rule of Sparky on page 97 for details about proper nouns and capitalization.

Nouns can appear anywhere in a sentence. However, the subject of a sentence always contains either a noun or pronoun (see pages 95-96.)

Pronoun—A pronoun is a word used in place of a noun or another pronoun in a sentence. *I, he, we, everyone,* and *someone* are examples of pronouns. There are different types of pronouns, just as there are different types of nouns. A **personal pronoun** takes the place of persons or things: *I, you, he, she, it, we, they.* **Possessive pronouns** show ownership. These include words like *my, mine, your, yours, his, her, hers, our, ours, their,* and *theirs.*

Most nouns are actual physical objects or people that can be heard, seen, touched, smelled, or tasted. These are called **concrete nouns**. Can you eat pizza? Yes, so pizza *is a concrete noun. So are* Idaho *and* nutmeg. *There are some nouns, like* happiness *and* philosophy, *that cannot be perceived using the five senses. These are* **abstract nouns**. Love *and* hate *are good examples. Concrete nouns will be the focus at the kindergarten through second-grade level.*

There are other forms of pronouns as well, but don't worry your child about these yet. For now, the key at this basic level is to get your child to understand that pronouns act as a substitute for a noun or another pronoun.

EXAMPLE:

Underline the correct pronoun:

Thomas liked to pack (his/their) own lunch.

My sister and I went to (my/our) home right after school.

In the first sentence, Thomas is only one person, so your child should pick *his,* since it is the singular pronoun. In the second sentence, though, there are two people (*my sister* and *I*), so the correct answer is *our.*

Verb—Verbs are words that express action, occurrence, or state of being. *Run, am,* and *laughed* are all verbs. There are two main types of verbs: action verbs and linking verbs. **Action verbs**, as you might expect, express an action that someone or something is taking. "Leo runs fast" contains the action verb *runs.* A **linking verb** does not express action; instead, it links the subject with other words that define the subject of the sentence. "Susan is my friend" contains the verb *is,* but it does nothing except link the word *Susan* to the words *my friend.* Common linking verbs often include a form of the verb *to be,* or are related to the senses (*look, feel*) or a state of being (*seem, become*).

Verbs can appear in more than one place in a sentence, but there is always at least one verb in the predicate of a sentence (see page 95).

The tense of a verb refers to time and duration of the action. At the kindergarten through second-grade level, your child will learn about the most basic, or simple, tense. The **simple tense** of a verb indicates that an event is present, past, or future in relation to the speaker:

- Present tense: *I write this book.*

- Past tense: *I ate roast beef yesterday for lunch.*

- Future tense: *I will call my mother tomorrow.*

EXAMPLE:

The silver turtle crawled slowly along the beach.

1) Draw a line between the subject and the predicate.
2) Circle the noun or pronoun in the subject.
3) Underline the verb in the predicate.

---

*There are some other verb tenses that your child might be exposed to by the second grade. The **perfect tense** of a verb indicates an action or condition that was or will be completed before another action or time. Verbs in the perfect tense are formed with the addition of* have *or* had *(I had walked this path as a child). The **progressive tense** of a verb shows an ongoing action in progress at some point in time; it uses some form of the verb* to be *(I am sleeping).*

For this sentence, the part that is doing the action—the subject—is *the silver turtle.* To help your child find the noun, ask him which of those three words describes a person, place, or thing. The noun is *turtle.* Your child might want to say that *silver* is a noun. If so, ask him what is doing the action in the sentence. Is *silver* doing something? No. The actor in the sentence is *turtle.*

The predicate of this sentence is *crawled slowly along the beach.* The one word that describes action, *crawled,* is the verb.

Adjective—Adjectives are words that describe or modify a noun or pronoun. The word *modify* means "limits" or "restricts." For example, in the sentence, "That red, four-door car in the parking lot is mine," the adjectives *red* and *four-door* modify the word *car,* limiting the number of cars in the parking lot that could be *mine.* Adjectives usually answer these questions: Which One? What kind? How many? *Red* and *four-door* help answer the question, "Which car is mine?"

Adverb—Adverbs are words that modify a verb, adjective, or another adverb. Adverbs answer questions like: How? How much? Where? When? Many adverbs are created by taking an adjective, like *slow*, and adding *-ly* to it to make the adverb *slowly*. In the sentence, "The rollercoaster moved quickly," the word *quickly* modifies the word *moved*. In the sentence, "He calls often," *often* describes how frequently he calls.

*The words a, an, and the are a group of adjectives known as **articles**. The word the refers to a specific person, place, or thing, so it is usually called a **definite article**. The words a or an refer to general nouns, so they are called **indefinite articles**.*

EXAMPLE:

The silver turtle crawled slowly along the beach.

1) Underline the adjectives.

2) Circle the noun or pronoun in the subject.

3) Double underline any articles.

In the English language, adjectives usually appear before a noun or pronoun, while adverbs appear after the word they modify. This fact allows your child to make a good guess if he comes to a word and he's not sure whether it is an adjective or an adverb. Have him find the word being modified, and if the unknown word is before it, guess "adjective." If it appears after the word it modifies, guess "adverb."

At last, the mystery of the word *silver* can be solved. Since it modifies the noun *turtle*, it is an adjective. *Slowly* modifies the verb *crawled* in this sentence, so it is an adverb. The definite article *the* appears twice.

Preposition—Prepositions are words that usually show the relationship between a noun or pronoun and other words in the sentence. *By, into, on, between,* and *for* are all prepositions.

Conjunction—Conjunctions are words used to combine or connect words or groups of words together. *And* and *but* are two of the most common conjunctions. *Or, nor, for,* and *yet* are also common conjunctions.

In the second grade, conjunctions might make an appearance if your child reaches the topic of **compound subjects** and **predicates**. A compound sentence features more than one noun in the subject. You can see this in the sentence *My sister and I went to our home right after school.* The subject contains both the noun *sister* and the pronoun *I.* Both words tell what the sentence is about.

For a compound predicate, let's go back to our favorite turtle. We know by now that the silver turtle crawled slowly along the beach. What if he also slipped? We would then have a sentence with a com-

Homework Heroics: Construct-A-Sentence

TWO PLAYER MINIMUM.

The Object: String together the longest sentence possible.

1) Player 1 supplies a noun (pelican), then player 2 supplies a verb (flies).

2) This noun and verb become the start of the sentence.

3) Player 1 now chooses one of the eight parts of speech (or just the first five described on the previous pages). Let's say player 1 picks "Adjective." Player 2 must now correctly add an adjective (spotted) to the sentence, and then repeat the sentence. (The spotted pelican flies.)

4) Player 2 now picks a part of speech, which player 1 must add correctly to the sentence. Player 1 must repeat the slightly longer sentence correctly.

5) Sometimes a player will have to add some additional words in order for the sentence to make sense. For example, you can't just add a conjunction; if you add a conjunction, you have to add at least one other word in order for the sentence to be grammatically correct. Quite often, you might have to add articles such as a, an, and the.

6) Play continues until someone adds a part of speech incorrectly—for example, by using an adverb to modify a noun—or if someone repeats the sentence incorrectly.

7) Make the sentences as silly as possible!

A good way to think about interjections is to combine them with exclamatory sentences (page 99). Both interjections and exclamatory sentences show feeling and emotion, and both are often proceeded by an exclamation mark.

pound predicate: The silver turtle crawled and slipped slowly along the beach.

Interjection—Interjections are words that express excitement and emotion. Interjections are often separated from a sentence by an exclamation point, or by a comma when the feeling's not as forceful. In the sentence, "Ouch! That stings," the interjection *ouch* shows it really did sting. Words like *alas, yikes, hey,* and *wow* are also interjections.

Basic drills on the eight parts of speech will occur throughout your child's schooling. Don't worry about the last three parts of speech at this time: your child should concentrate on recognizing nouns, pronouns, verbs, adjectives, and adverbs.

Reading

As stated at the beginning of this chapter, encouraging your child to read will help her learn the English language in many ways. Certainly, developing a love for reading will come in handy when she has to create her first book report. Who knows? She might even become the first student to actually read the book, and not just the jacket cover. We're kidding!

But before the book reports start popping up in later grades, your child will have to learn the basics of reading comprehension. Your child will learn not only the meaning of the sentences she reads, but what they mean when combined to form a six- or eight- sentence paragraph. To do this, she will have to understand things like sequence of events, characters, setting, and some other basic ideas. This section will talk about these concepts in both fiction and nonfiction writing.

First, though, here's a brief discussion of the difference between these two types of writing.

Nonfiction is factual writing. News articles, essays, history books, biographies, almanacs, reference materials—anything that does not involve making up people, places, and events—is nonfiction.

Fiction is a class of writing that involves narration in prose form (meaning that it's not poetry) and deals with partly or completely imaginary characters or events. Here's a simple equation to help sort things out:

·····

Fiction = Someone Made it Up

·····

So if a boy tells his parents that he didn't complete his homework because he was playing, that's nonfiction. But if the boy claims that aliens landed just after he finished his homework and took his assignment with them into space, that's fiction.

Now your child will understand the importance of writing good fiction.

Understanding both nonfiction and fiction writing requires a knowledge of certain concepts. Here is a review of some key terms.

Key Idea: Character and Setting

Here is a sample paragraph of nonfiction writing to help illustrate characters and setting:

My family went hiking this weekend. The weather was cold in the morning. In the afternoon it was hot. I ended up sweating up a lot. I was tired by the time I reached the top of the mountain. The view from the top was beautiful. It was definitely worth all the trouble.

Characters—These are the people (and/or creatures) within a story. In this nonfiction piece, the **main character** is the child. He is the person around whom the action revolves. However, he is not only the only character: the main character's family is also mentioned. Since the family doesn't play a large role in the piece, they are considered **minor characters**. Sometimes, the phrase **supporting characters** is used in place of minor characters. They both mean the same thing, but the phrase *supporting characters* shows how these parts "support" the main character.

First-person stories are the easiest to understand in terms of characters, because the person doing the talking is the main character. Your child can rewrite the story to change this. Read the following nonfiction account.

> Today, our next-door neighbors, Frank and Brigit, went hiking. The weather was cold in the morning. In the afternoon it was hot. They returned around 4:00 P.M. I went to talk to Frank and Brigit. Frank said he was tired by the time he reached the top of the mountain. Brigit agreed. They both said the view from the top was beautiful.

EXAMPLE:

Who are the characters in this account?

This is essentially the same story, but the characters have changed. There are two named characters, Frank and Brigit, as well as the **narrator**, or the person who is telling the story. (In this example, the narrator is just relating the story, but in the first version of the story the narrator is also the main character.) You could make a case that Frank's and Brigit's parents are also characters, but that's more of a guess since they are not specifically mentioned.

In addition to just knowing the names of the characters, your child's comprehension will increase if he can understand, or relate to, the characters. What are the character's feelings, motives, and actions?

Most writing will provide clues that a reader can use in order to get to know the characters better, and even "feel" the same way they feel.

EXAMPLE:

How does the speaker feel at the end of the story on page 112?

A. cold

B. angry

C. thrilled

D. bored

In the second grade, your child might be asked to start comparing two characters, explaining how they are alike and how they are different. For example, suppose that Brigit didn't enjoy the view from the top of the mountain. This would mean that she and her brother Frank had some similarities (they both climbed the mountain) and some differences (Frank enjoyed it, but Brigit didn't).

Choice A is incorrect (and kind of tricky) because although it was cold in the morning, it warmed up. Choices B and D are incorrect, as well; there's no indication in the story that he was upset or uninterested. The correct answer is C, because the view from the top was so beautiful. Your child needs to understand the different feelings of the character in order to understand the story itself.

Setting—Setting is the location, scenery, or period of time in which a story or other work takes place.

Many times, the setting of a story affects the **mood**. Mood is the emotional atmosphere of the piece. If you accidentally hit your hand with a hammer, your mood will probably be a bad, or angry, one, but if you win the lottery, your mood would most likely be joyous. In stories, setting can influence the mood. For example, if a story takes place on a sinking skip, the mood would be one of anxiety or nervousness.

Characters, setting, and mood are all interconnected—shouting, arguing characters create a mood of anger, for example—and can help your child understand what's taking place. By answering basic questions, such as "Who are the characters?" and "Where does the story take place?" or "What was the mood of the main character?" your child should improve his reading comprehension.

Key Idea: Sequence of Events and the Main Idea

Sequence of Events—Understanding the order in which events occur in a story is an important concept in reading comprehension, and your child will probably spend a lot of time on it at the kindergarten through second-grade level.

EXAMPLE:

Place the number 1, 2, or 3 next to these events in the order they occurred in the second story.

The narrator went to talk to his friends.

Frank and Brigit climbed the mountain.

Frank and Brigit looked from the mountain-top.

The correct answer for the question above is 2, 3, 1. If your child is having trouble on assignments that require sequencing events, have her make a list when reading the story, writing a brief summary of important events as they occur. The list should help her focus on the action of the story and improve her concentration skills.

Homework Heroics: Understanding Sequence

TO HELP YOUR child develop an understanding of the sequence of events, you can have her write out a list of what she does to prepare for school each morning. Does she eat breakfast before getting out of bed? Does she put on her school clothes and then take a shower? If she does, then kids are going to laugh at that squeaky sound her shoes make when they're leaking water.

Main Idea—Most stories, nonfiction or fiction, aren't merely ramblings with no point. They have a main idea, which is the central message of the piece. Understanding the main idea of a story is like providing a frame and canvas for a painting: you still have to fill in all the details, but at least you have an inkling of the overall picture. For example, the main idea in the first hiking story would be something like, "A child climbs up a mountain and finds the view wonderful."

Once your child understands the main idea, she can sometimes makes predictions, or inferences, based on information found in the piece.

EXAMPLE:

Do you think the main character in the first story (see page 112) would like to go hiking again?

By understanding the story, your child can now take a mental leap and make a prediction. This is moving away from focusing on what's written specifically on the page and involves doing some independent thinking, a great step in terms of reading comprehension. The answer to this question is most likely "Yes." Your child should come to this conclusion because the narrator in the story was so impressed with the view from the top.

Homework Heroics: Summarizing

A GREAT PLACE to find main ideas is a television guide. Local or national, a television guide will summarize the movies and television programs being shown, often in one sentence or two. You can watch a movie or television show with your child, and then ask her to summarize it in her own words. Or, if your child has already seen the movie or program, you can skip the viewing part and just go straight to the main idea stage. This way is faster, but it doesn't involve that favorite pastime: making popcorn.

Key Idea: Who, What, When, Where, Why, and How?

While terms like character, setting, and sequence are all helpful ways to build reading comprehension skills, they are by no means the only way. Another good model to try is the "Six Questions" approach: Who, What, When, Where, Why, and How. By asking, and then answering, these six questions, your child will better be able to understand a piece of writing.

By now you might have the hiking story memorized, but if your child had to read it for a homework assignment, you could ask her these types of questions to increase her comprehension of the piece:

1) Who is climbing the mountain?

2) What occurs at the end of the story? At the beginning?

3) When do the events take place?

4) Where do the events occur?

5) Why was it worth the climb?

6) How does the story end?

As you can see, the Six Questions model has many similarities to the ideas discussed on pages 112-117. For example, question 1 defines all the characters, while questions 2 and 3 discuss the sequence of events. If your child prefers thinking in terms of Who, What, When, Where, Why, and How, by all means let her do so. It is a proven, effective approach to reading comprehension.

Of course, these are not the only questions that could be asked. Question 6 could be restated to say, "How does the story *begin*?" In each instance, however, the answer to the question clarifies a portion of the story. The more questions your child can ask and answer about the story, the better her understanding of the story will be.

Writing

Many of the concepts discussed in the previous section, Reading, are also relevant to this section. This is because if your child is writing a fiction piece, he will need to provide characters, setting, a sequence of events, and an overall theme, or main idea. If he doesn't, then his story will be difficult or even impossible to understand. The focus, then, at the kindergarten through second-grade level, will be on learning how to write a story that has a beginning, a middle, and an end.

Key Idea: Writing Fiction

At the early stages, your child won't be asked to write an entire story from scratch. Instead, the goal will be to complete a story, like

---

EXAMPLE:

Write a final sentence for this story:

The dolphin swam lazily in the bay. Out of the corner of its eye, it noticed a school of fish swimming for the open sea. The dolphin kicked its powerful fin and started swimming. It raced towards the school of fish. _____

So, what happens next? It is up to your child to decide, but there are three main possibilities:

1) The dolphin caught some fish.

2) The dolphin didn't catch some fish.

3) The dolphin decided to swim with the fish.

Your child could write a fourth option, but it probably wouldn't have much to do with what is already written.

Given a beginning, a middle, a setting, and a character (the dolphin), your child had only to provide the final stage of the sequence of events. As her fiction writing skill improves, the writing prompts will provide less and less prompting material at the beginning, leaving more to your child's imagination.

EXAMPLE:

Write a short story (4-6 sentences) about a dolphin swimming in a bay.

In this instance, your child is given a character (dolphin) and a setting (bay), but that's it. Her goals would be to decide the sequence of events and the overall theme (see pages 115-116 for more on these topics). Perhaps this theme will be different from "A dolphin chases fish." It could be a spy thriller! "A dolphin works for the Navy defusing mines."

If she doesn't know where to start writing, ask her to talk about her unformed story, using the elements discussed throughout the Reading section. Is the dolphin the only character? What is the mood of the story? How will you portray the action in the story?

As your child answers these questions, her story will take form. Your job is merely to prompt her in defining the action and characters.

Key Idea: Writing Nonfiction

In addition to all the elements of writing already discussed, the key to good nonfiction writing (and good fiction writing, too, for that matter) is **detail**. The more details, or supporting statements, your child provides will usually translate into a better, more descriptive piece of writing.

EXAMPLE:

Write a brief paragraph about how you spent your weekend.

This question could be answered, "I went to the zoo." This is factual, but it's not a paragraph and it's not very interesting, either. In other words, it is nonfiction, but it isn't good nonfiction.

To make it better, your child should add more details about what he did while at the zoo. What animals did he see? Which animal did he like the most? Did he enjoy the trip? Did any polar bears escape and raid the ice-cream truck? By taking the answers to these questions and then placing them in the proper sequence, your child can write a nonfiction paragraph that is interesting and descriptive. For example:

> This Saturday I went to the zoo with my younger brother. We saw hundreds of animals. I liked the hippos best, but my brother enjoyed the snake farm the most. He's such a weirdo! We had lunch near the birdhouses around noon. At three o' clock we went home. I spent the rest of the weekend doing chores and talking with friends.

The sentence, "He's such a weirdo!" helps the reader understand two characters, the brother (he likes cold, slimy reptiles) and the narrator (he thinks people who likes snakes are strange.)

The increase in detail transformed a sentence that wasn't very interesting into a well-written, descriptive paragraph.

CHAPTER 4

A Review of Basic K-2 Science and Social Studies Concepts

THE BULK OF YOUR CHILD'S EDUCA-TION at the kindergarten through second-grade level will fall under the Math and English Language Arts categories. However, your child may be introduced to some basic science and social studies skills, so this chapter provides a brief overview of some of the concepts they are likely to learn. Some of the skills discussed in this section, such as categorizing objects, might fall under "Basic Thinking Skills" in some states.

Science

Key Idea: Scientific Observation

The recording and analysis of data is important for scientific experimentation. At this level, your child will be taught about the various types of scientific measuring equipment and how they are used. However, many of the more advanced scientific instruments, such as the microscope and scales, probably will not be used until the second grade, or later. Homework assignments focusing on these instruments often involve simply understanding what each object does.

Common Scientific Tools	What It Does
Microscope	Magnifies objects, making them appear larger
Scale	Weighs objects (or compares the weight of two objects)
Ruler (metric and standard)	Measures the length of objects
Thermometer	Measures the temperature

At the kindergarten through second-grade level, your child will probably use the ruler more than any other scientific instrument. Keep in mind that even using a ruler is not something that every youngster gets right away, so it's worth working on measuring assignments with your child to make sure he knows how to align the ruler correctly.

All of these are standard scientific instruments. Using them, your child could answer the following question.

EXAMPLE:

Find two rocks. Compare the length, weight, and color of the rocks.

To compare weight, your child would use the scales. He would use the ruler to measure the lengths of the rocks. For the color, he would use his eyes, a powerful scientific tool that he can take anywhere. If he wants to examine each rock up close, he could place them under a microscope.

Afterwards, he could even place the results in a chart (for more about charts, see pages 81-83).

	Length	Weight	Color
Rock 1	4 inches	1 pound	black
Rock 2	6 inches	12 ounces	grayish

Conclusion: Rock 1 weighs more, but Rock 2 is longer.

Although this assignment is simple, it has a sound scientific underpinning. Even Nobel-prize research follows a similar procedure (they just use fancier words):

1) Examination with scientific instruments

2) Writing up the results (data)

3) Drawing a conclusion

Sadly, the rock analysis probably won't get picked by the Nobel prize committee. But it's good work, nevertheless.

Key Idea: Basic Safety Procedures

This could also be titled, "Don't Eat the Bugs That You're Analyzing," or "Don't Use Rock 1 to Try and Crush Rock 2." Seriously, proper use of scientific equipment is the focus here, especially when it enhances the safety of

The study of rocks and minerals is known as geology. Your child might have some basic geology questions like this one, showing how some rocks look different and have different properties. For example, pumice is a light, powdery rock, while marble is a much heavier rock that retains a good polish. With this in mind, ask your child: would you rather have a house built out of marble or pumice? Which one would make a strong building, and which one would constantly be eroded by the wind and rain?

your child and the classroom. Learning how to carry scissors correctly, or to wash her hands after handling scientific material, are essential safety rules that younger students will need to know.

Your child will probably also be taught how to extinguish oxygen-based combustion involving flames. Of course, it won't be called that at your child's school—they'll just say, "This is how to put out a fire." This is useful information in a science lab, and for life in general.

•••••

Tell your child that if part of her clothing catches fire, the best action is to stop, drop, and roll.

•••••

Don't worry—flammable experiments are not part of a kinder-garten through second-grade curricula, but the safety measures are often discussed at this grade because they are so important.

Key Idea: Properties of Matter

The three main states of matter are solid, liquid, and gas. Your child will not have to define these states—he will only have to recognize them.

Solid—A solid holds its own shape.

Liquid—A liquid is a state between a solid and a gas. It has substance (or volume), but it doesn't have a set shape; it takes the shape of the container it is in.

Gas—Gas particles can rarely be seen, and they have no definite shape or substance. Gas expands or contracts to fill the container into which it is placed.

A balloon is a good way to illustrate the three states of matter. The balloon itself is a solid (but very flexible) piece of rubber or plastic. If you blow air into it, the balloon expands, but it holds its own shape. It's still the same shape, although it is stretched out.

The air inside the balloon is a gas, because it has no definite substance and it expands to fill the shape of the balloon. Let the air out, and now fill the balloon with water. Explain to your child that water is a liquid, because it has substance and it takes the shape of the balloon.

Key Idea: Motion and Energy

At this juncture in your child's education, the concept of motion largely involves studying objects that are moving and drawing some conclusion from them. For example, your child might be given the following question:

EXAMPLE:

How can you make a baseball move?

Your child might answer:

1) push it

2) pull it

3) hit it with a bat

4) drop it off a building

5) blow on it

> *Idea 4 employs the use of **gravity**, which is a force that affects all terrestrial objects, pulling them toward an imaginary point at the center of the earth.*

All of these are acceptable answers, and no further explanation is needed. Your child might also be asked to explain how some of the answers are related. For example, answers 3 and 5 are similar; in both cases, the baseball is struck by something. In answer 3, the object doing the striking is a solid (a bat), while for answer 5, the object "striking" the baseball is a gas (your child's breath.) Neat, eh?

Energy comes in many different forms, and while your child does not have to know them all, it is helpful if she knows some basic forms of energy.

Basic Forms of Energy

Energy Type	Example
Solar	Sunlight
Electrical	Lightning
Chemical	A fire; the reaction of chemicals within a battery that produces an electric current

Electrical energy is also called **electromagnetic energy**, since anything that carries an electrical current creates a magnetic field. The two ideas, electricity and magnetism, are intricately linked in a way your child will not have to understand for a while. Since electricty is invisible for the most part (lightning is a notable exception), magnets provide a way to show your child about how electricity does carry force. Take two refrigerator magnets and try to place them together. There should be some resistance. This is one example of an electromagnetic force.

Key Idea: Simple Machines

A machine is something that makes work easier to do. For example, lifting a heavy box straight off the ground to place on a table can be difficult. It is easier to slide the heavy box up a ramp to the top of the table. The ramp, or **inclined plane**, is a simple machine. Other simple machines include:

Lever—The best example of a lever is a see-saw. The see-saw is a lever that allows people at both ends to lift one another up and down. The lever, or see-saw, is balanced on top of a **fulcrum**.

Wedge—Imagine using the back of an axe to try to cut into a tree. It wouldn't be very effective, since this end is blunt and unable to pierce the bark. However, if you use the sharp edge of the axe, the blade sinks in. This is an example of using a wedge—usually a triangular shape—to do work.

Screw—Why are screws effective? In essence, they are like nails with a long, curving inclined plane wrapped along their length. This "spiral groove" allows screws to penetrate material such as wood. This outer wedge then keeps the screw in place.

Pulley—A simple pulley consists of a grooved wheel with a rope attached over the top. A construction crane is a good example. The crane functions as a huge pulley: heavy things are attached to its hook, which is connected to a rope that goes to the top of the crane's arm. This allows objects to be lifted and moved.

Wheel-and-Axle—One form of wheel-and-axle combination consists of two wheels connected on a rod on which the wheels spin. Imagine a car with no wheels. It would be hard to push along a street, wouldn't it? However, by adding wheels and axles, the car is now easier to move.

Simple machines give young children a good introduction to simple physics. Before burdening them with equations like, work = force × distance, children need to understand how moving an object takes effort, and that simple machines can be used to make some jobs easier.

Key Idea: Cataloging Events or Objects

Science assignments dealing with cataloging events or objects most frequently involve the question, "Which of these is not like the other?" Sometimes the answer is obvious, as in an example that has pictures of four different kinds of food and then a picture of a house. At other times, there isn't one correct answer. What's important is the logic your child uses to explain his answer.

EXAMPLE:

Which of these animals does not fit in with the rest?

Your child must now look at the four pictures and decide on some cataloging system. If he chooses "land-based animals," then the dolphin is definitely the odd creature out. If the system is "animals without flippers," then the dolphin is out of luck again.

However, for this question there is not one absolute answer. For example, what if your child decided to use the category, "animals that cannot fly"? That would mean that the bird is excluded, since it can fly. So the key to cataloging questions is not to find the one exact answer, but to make sure that your child's answer matches up properly with the category he creates, and that he can explain his reasoning.

Categorizing objects is an important skill because in science, everything is categorized. Plants are categorized; rocks are categorized; planets and solar systems are categorized; even dogs are categorized. With this in mind, you can see how categorizing skills will come in handy.

Key Idea: Technology and Our Society

The gist of this subject is that scientific inventions change human society and the environment. Although your child wasn't around during the time of the horse-drawn buggy, she should be able to see that the invention of the automobile has changed many things in the world. Questions in this category will be this broad: there's no need to worry about anything but the Big Picture.

EXAMPLE:

List some ways in which recycling helps the environment.

This question only focuses on whether your child understands the concept of recycling. The correct answer can be something along the lines of, "Recycling paper helps preserve trees and forests. If paper is recycled, then people don't have to cut down more trees in order to make new paper; they can make recycled paper instead."

Similar big topics that your child might be asked to explain include:

1) The invention of the telephone/telegraph

2) The passenger airplane

3) The invention of the printing press

4) The birth of Rock 'n' Roll!

Okay, that last category is not exactly a technological event, but it was time to liven things up a little. The key to helping your child with these kinds of questions is to ask leading questions, such as, "For what kinds of things do we use the telephone? How do you think people handled those tasks prior to the invention of the telephone? Do you think people could travel from Ohio to California to visit grandma before planes were invented?" These types of questions will help your child understand the importance of technological inventions.

Social Studies

Much of what your young child will learn under the category of Social Studies involves fun stuff—like making dioramas or making turkey shapes by tracing the palms of their hands—and very little memorization of facts. Here are brief descriptions of a few topics that are likely to surface.

Key Idea: Citizenship

This involves questions about what laws are, and why it is bad to break them. Your child might be asked, "Why is speeding in a car dangerous?" Your child would be expected to answer with something like, "Speeding causes accidents, which is why there is a law against it. Laws are meant to protect people from injury or harm. Being a good citizen means that you follow these rules."

Classroom citizenship is also a key concept in kindergarten through second grade. Your child will be taught to treat other children with respect, to line up before going to recess, and to raise her hand before speaking. These basic rules help your child understand citizenship in the classroom, but citizenship lessons will also deal with larger social courtesies. In other words, your child will learn about politeness, and when to say "thank you" and "you're welcome." Other social citizenship issues involve how to have polite converstations, the importance of listening and not interrupting, and maintaining eye contact when speaking.

Although your child may have posters of his favorite athletes over every square inch of wall space, suggest that he find room for a good world map. It's almost like learning through osmosis: humans are visual creatures, and your child will invariably be drawn to the map from time to time. You would be surprised at how much geographic knowledge can be absorbed just by hanging a map in a prominent location.

One way to give your child some practice in this area is to let them watch any daytime talk show. Then, when it is over, turn to them and say, "That is exactly how *not* to behave."

Key Idea: Geography

Your child should be able to spot the following three places on a globe or map:

1) The continent on which he lives, North America

2) The country in which he lives, the United States

3) The state (and maybe even the city) in which he lives

Key Idea: Holidays

What's the most important thing about a holiday? No school! Seriously, your child's teacher will probably spend some time explaining the major holidays and their significance. For example, your child might learn that July 4th is celebrated as the day our nation declared its independence from England. Holidays, therefore, can provide a historical nugget of information that your child can build on in later years, when thorough discussion of such events as the American Revolution begins.

Most of the homework at this level will involve creating cards or pictures to commemorate a particular holiday or important individual in American history. You might be called on to help with scissors, glue, and glitter for these homework assignments.

Key Idea: Symbols of the United States

Symbols like the American flag, the Statue of Liberty, and figures from American legends or folklore (such as George Washington chopping down the cherry tree) provide valuable information about our country. For example, when studying the American flag, your child will learn that there are currently fifty stars, one for each state in the union. The stars and stripes, and the colors on the flag were also chosen for a reason, and understanding the meaning behind the flag—and other symbols—teaches your child important aspects of the nation's heritage. Your child will likely learn about her state symbols and flag as well.

CHAPTER 5

A Final Word

 MANY STUDENTS WILL NEED HELP on topics that fall outside of the major areas covered in this book. If your child is taking fencing lessons, for example, we really have not given you any pointers to pass on to him. Okay, here's one—keep your elbow extended when lunging—but that's it. Our fencing days are over.

In this case, and in others, you won't be able to impart the correct knowledge to your child at a moment's notice. But regardless of the subject matter, when your child asks you for help on his homework, you can always be supportive, caring, and kind when answering. If you don't know the answer, try working with your child to search for the answer. Remember, it's important that you try not to get frustrated and upset, because your child picks up on your attitudes and feelings about homework. Keep in mind there's a larger issue at stake, which is the relationship between you and your child.

Mutual caring and respect between the two of you will always be more important than any one fact, so if you find yourself losing your composure because you and your child cannot find out what year the Treaty of Ghent was signed, don't get upset. Reassure your child that homework doesn't have to be perfect every time, and you can learn from your mistakes as well. This positive, caring attitude—more than any one fact—is what will make you a Homework Hero in the eyes of your child.

By the way, the Treaty of Ghent was signed in 1814.

Homework on the World Wide Web

If you have a computer with an Internet connection, you might like to take a peek at these homework-related sites:

Bigchalk.com
http://www.bigchalk.com

B.J. Pinchbeck's Homework Helper
http://school.discovery.com/homeworkhelp/bjpinchbeck/index.html

Dictionary.com
http://www.dictionary.com

DiscoverySchool.com
http://school.discovery.com/students/

Fact Monster.com
http://www.factmonster.com/homework/

Homeworkspot.com
http://www.homeworkspot.com/

Thesaurus.com
http://www.thesaurus.com/

Yahooligans! School Bell: Homework Help
http://www.yahooligans.com/school_bell/homework_help/

Information for parents of children with learning differences
http://www.SchwabLearning.com

Other Books by Priscilla L. Vail, M.A.T.

A Language Yardstick: Understanding and Assessment
About Dyslexia: Unraveling the Myth
Clear and Lively Writing: Language Games and Activities for Everyone
Common Ground: Phonics and Whole Language Working Together
Emotion: The On/Off Switch for Learning
Gifted, Precocious, or Just Plain Smart
Learning Styles: Food for Thought and 130 Practical Tips
Reading Comprehension: Students' Needs and Teachers' Tools
Smart Kids with School Problems: Things to Know and Ways to Help
Third and Fourth Grade Language Assessment
Words Fail Me!: How Language Works and What Happens When It Doesn't
The World of the Gifted Child

Acknowledgements

Drew and Cynthia Johnson would like to thank their friends—Frank, Jeff, Renee, John, Sam, and Kelly—at Magnolia Café South and Vulcan Video South for keeping them well-fed and visually entertained during the course of writing this book.